The Reluctant Duke

By

Antonino d'Este

The old Duke bypasses his two sons and chooses one of his nephews to succeed him to the ducal title of the House of Este. The nephew is not certain he wants the honor.

_____

Copyright 1999 by Antonino d'Este

All rights reserved. No part of this book may be used or reproduced in any manner whatsoever without written permission, except in the case of brief quotations embodied in critical articles or reviews.

The Reluctant Duke
Published 1999

Printed in the United States of America

ISBN 978-0-578-00476-1

Dedicated to

The Estensi,

The house of Este

Crest of the House of Este,

A Princely family of Lombard origin,
That played a great part in the history
Of Medieval and Renaissance Italy.

Motto: Without hope, Without Fear

Books by Antonino d'Este
******

An American Duke
An American Sheik
I'll Tell You When the Night Comes
An American Duke in Italy
Duchinos and Duchessinas
Secrets of a Bounty Hunter
The Real Lucrezia Borgia
Clear the Bridge! Dive! Dive!
Kings without Crowns
The Reluctant Duke
I'll Think About It
The Diary of Gilda d'Este Colonna
Extended Family
The Money Rats
Commoner Marriage
Murder at the Altar
The Dilemma of Love
One Day Before Tomorrow

List of People in this book

The author, Antonino d'Este
"Vince" d'Este, my nephew.
    Gilda Colonna, his wife.
    Maria, their daughter
    Piero, their son.
Vincenti d'Este, my eldest son, the 'Malandrino'
    Regina, his wife.
    Leonello, their only son.
    Nino, her second son. (Fathered by Vince.)
    Luciano, her third son, (Fathered by "Terzo")
Isabella, my first daughter, became a Nun
Beatrice, my second daughter.
    Francesco della Rovere, her husband
Antonino III (Terzo), and Lucrezia, my twins
    Damiano Villano, her husband
Leonora, my last daughter, "The baby"
    Andrea di Savoia, her husband.
    Isabella, their daughter. (Fathered by Vince.)
Tinti Fusco, my ward, became Princess Palavicino
    Prince Nocolo Palavicino, her husband.
Elena, my niece.
    Her sister Monica, a Nun,
Deli al Aziz, a Syrian girl taken into the Castello,
    Armal al Aziz, her son. (Fathered by Vince.)
Marco di Dante, the new household secretary.

Aurelia, his wife
Velia, Secretary Marco's assistant.
Count Giulio Villano, mentor and friend of the author, and Damiano's father.
Father Alessi, the family priest.
Michele, family chauffeur and former policeman.
Andrea Astuzia, the family mechanic
The Bergamo Gang:
- Salvatore Mancuso, the boss.
- Angelo Costa, his lieutenant.
- Santo Citterio
- Abbruzzi Faro, "L'imbicile"

Foreword.

After the death of my wife, The Duchess Laura, I became dispirited, and no longer wanted to continue living in Italy. I returned to my native New York City and after a time went into semi-retirement in Saint Petersburg, Florida. All this is told in my book "An American Duke in Italy".

I left the running of the household and the business in Italy in the hands of my first-born son Vincenti, the rightful heir to the ducal title, thinking he would take an active part in tending to the family, the land and the Castello.

Instead, Vincenti and his wife Regina chose to live in the palazzo in Milano, and to enjoy the life in that city, neglecting his duties to the family and its interests. After he ignored several of my warnings, and my second son Antonino Terzo being unsuitable to the task, I began to look around in the family for a suitable replacement for the ducal succession.

My eyes fell on Vince, the second son of my brother Piero. He was working as a Bounty Hunter, and had all the attributes to be a good Duke: courage, toughness, independence, and innovative thinking.

I called him to Florida, and our discussions began. At first I became fascinated by the stories of his adventures as a Bounty Hunter, and I asked him to give me all of his notes. These led to my writing my book, "Secrets of a Bounty Hunter."

It soon became evident that my nephew would make a good candidate to be named to the succession. I would be comfortable if he became the next head of the family.

I said nothing to him then. I wanted to move cautiously, getting him to like Italy, and the family there, before I sprung my idea on him.

When I did, he wasn't thrilled at the prospect.

Vince,

The New Duke

Opinions

The family before all others,
Is the saving grace
For the good health and safety
Of the individual person who lives
Within that family structure.

Duke Antonino d'Este
****

I am not a believer
In such things.
The individual must step out,
And serve himself.
This is his best chance
At true self-discovery
Within the family of man.

Vince d'Este

Chapter One

A difficult decision

Some people may say that I told my nephew Vince a white lie when I asked him to accompany me to Italy. It's true that I did withhold my full intention, but that's not the same as lying.

Suggesting he think of it as a vacation was not misleading either. I wasn't sure if I would select him for the succession, so at that time I thought there was no sense in saying too much about it.

It would be a difficult decision for me because my wife died thinking that naturally, our eldest son Vincenti would be the successor to the ducal title, and indeed that was my intention too. I wanted to be loyal to her sweet memory and tried in every way I knew to prepare Vincenti to step into my shoes.

When I realized the Vincenti would not be fit for the position I did not have any idea who might take his place. There was my second son, Antonino the Third, (or "Terzo" as he was called.) but he long ago showed no leadership qualities, and I never gave him a second thought.

So you see, when I asked Vince to come with me I was not sure of him either. I was in a quandary, and the thought of the family and the business structure falling apart from lack of leadership was unsettling.

Saving everything for the family was uppermost in my mind. If I failed in this last effort, then my whole life, all of the sacrifices I was called upon to make, and all the dangers I faced would have amounted to nothing.

The only answer was to find someone within the family who could shoulder the load and in effect save the family from its own indolent practices. A strong man was needed.

It was a bit of serendipity that Vince was, how to say, "between jobs", and was more than ready for a new adventure. He later said that he thought I wanted his company more as a bodyguard than anything else, so he never suspected where my true thoughts were going.

During the flight over and during our stay at the Castello, he stuck to me like glue. He even serrupticiously followed me down to the crypt where I visited my wife's coffin, and later told his father that he saw me crying over her casket.

I also learned that he later had made the recommendation to my daughter Leonora that the coffin be cleaned and polished every month. He had noticed the marks my hands made in the dust covering it.

This was one of the things that made me certain that he would be the one to take my place. His powers of observation and his thoroughness made it plain that he could do the work.

We traveled around and I showed Vince the extent of the family holdings, and I could see that he was impressed, but he showed no sign of any interest or venality. I was doing my best to lay the groundwork so that he had some idea of what was involved.

I didn't seem to be succeeding. He was watching ME, and not the property. How was I going to peak his interest in all of that? During our later conversations he told me that he thought I was just bragging about my accomplishments, still never suspecting that I wanted him to learn about the work involved...

What Vince really liked was what Terzo was doing to create "The Villa Laura" out of what was once a large, forlorn castle, the Castello Fuori near Neunkirchen, Austria. He remarked at what an undertaking it was after seeing pictures of the old edifice, and looking over the spread of the new villa, built practically from the old foundation, out.

"One can hardly believe that this is the same ground." he told Terzo, and my son could not help strutting around like a peacock. Vince was right. This was where Terzo's talent really lay, and this project was his plaything.

Terzo could play, but he could not lead. Laura and I were blessed with two fine sons, but the elder was a bit of wastrel, and the second ineffectual beyond his own reach.

All the while during the trip Vince stayed close to me. Not even my two Sicilian guards watched over me the way he did. He was intent on seeing me safe and back to my home in Florida, even if it meant his life. I was convinced of that.

I had put Vincenti and his wife Regina in the Fusco manor, and he was to take care of the house, the land and his immediate family. That wasn't exactly what he wanted, and I later learned he had connived to spend more time in Milano while no one was looking.

When Vince and I visited them on the Fusco land, Vincenti showed us around and explained what he was doing to make it a going concern, and he made it sound convincing. He had lived here before as punishment and as a way to redeem himself, and he did well at the time.

That experience helped him get right into the work, but his heart was not in it. Alas, a leopard does not change his spots, and his sneaky plan was later discovered.

Then I got sick and wound up in the same hospital in Monza where my wife died some seven years before. The family became alarmed and soon all family members that could make it to the Castello Estensi came there. Even my daughter Isabella, a nun living in a convent in Ferrara, got special permission from the Mother Superior to visit.

What I thought was a bad cold developed into pneumonia, and the family expected me to die. Vince stayed at the hospital every day, leaving only to sleep and eat, and blaming himself for not being able to protect me from illness.

The family marveled at Vince's loyalty and persistence, but none of them thought of him as the next Duke, but just a loyal nephew. Indeed, it was my son Vincenti who came to the Castello and started acting as though he were already in charge. He did not understand that his unacceptable behavior disqualified him.

After I started to recover, Vince told me of the dissention in the household. He said that Vincenti was barking orders, upsetting everyone, and even his wife Regina was behaving as though she were already the Duchess of the Castello.

Well, I could understand how she would think that. She did marry the Duchino Vincenti, and had every right to think she would be the Duchess when I passed away.

I asked the doctors what my prognosis was, and was assured by them that I had many good years left. I told Vince that Vincenti and Regina were in for a surprise, but still did not mention that I was considering him for the succession.

Yet being ill made me realize that I had to think about my own mortality, and that I'd better move up the timetable for the selection of the new Duke. At that time I felt that I was running out of time.

Even with this warning I still intended to retire, so it was only natural that I desired to put the whole business into someone else's capable hands. I decided then and there, lying in a hospital bed, that Vince would be named the next Duke.

I had to complete my recovery at the Castello after I was released from the hospital, so I asked Vince if he would mind the wait. He didn't, so we were able to spend some quality time together.

He told me how much he liked the interior appointments of the Castello, especially the building's showplace, the Crystal Room. "What a treat it would have been to see the artists at work, making this room into the incredible thing of beauty it had become."

I had to smile at his innocence. Little did he dream that someday it would all be his. Now I had to convince HIM to accept it when I finally told him of my plans.

Chapter Two

The plan revealed

"Vince, you must understand my problem," I told him, once we got back to my villa in Florida. "The logical and intended person to become the next Duke is my firstborn son, Vincenti, but he is intent on living a profligate life of ease and pleasure in Milano, and shows no interest in his duties to the family. I cannot allow all the work and heartache that went into the re-building of the family's wealth and position to wither on the vine while he and his wife indulge themselves in a life of indolence.

"I've decided to name you to the succession, and to have you move into the Castello and continue my work."

"Uncle", Vince responded, "I know nothing of the life in Italy, and I don't understand why you think I'll be capable of stepping into your shoes. All I do is play tennis and chase criminals. When I am not doing those things, I too am living a life of ease in New York City. Why do you think I'm suitable for such an important position?"

"There is no doubt in my mind. You will not be stepping into my shoes exactly. Once you are named Duke, you will know how to do things by using your own brains. You will have free reign, and I will be here to guide you. In fact, you will have more freedom than I did, because I was hindered by the original contract which prevented me from selling any of our holdings."

"Uncle, is this a free discussion? May I say what's on my mind?"

Of, course! That's exactly what I expect you to do."

"First, do I address you as 'Your Grace'?"

"No, not here in the United States. In Europe, we must observe the conventions, but between ourselves we must be comfortable, and share the kind of intimacy close relatives have. Start to think like the next Duke, and you will soon feel that we are coevals."

"That sounds good! Tell me, what's in all this for me? Would I be sacrificing myself to serve the family, or will I have a life I can call my own?"

"Vince, *I* was the sacrificial lamb. Most of your duties will involve maintenance more than anything else, but there are always the unexpected events that no one can predict. I'm depending on the ingenuity you have already demonstrated in your work as a Bounty Hunter to meet these problems. Other than that, you can live your life as you please, within certain boundaries."

"Ah! What are these boundaries?"

"You will be bound to honor some of the conditions in the old contract, like taking care of the Colonna family. They must continue to share in whatever wealth comes to the family. They are part of the family too. Remember, they are the relatives of the Duchess Laura. Her parents still live in the Castello. We must honor the contract, and her sainted memory."

"I certainly understand that. If I were to accept this responsibility, I would not go in with a wreaking ball. Still, I don't quiet understand why you think I qualify. Why can't Vincenti step in?"

"He wants to coast along without any responsibilities. Sadly, there are a lot of such young men in Italy today. I will not permit that to happen. He's going to work, one way or another. If he thinks otherwise he'll be in for some agonizing days in the future.

"I'm amazed he doesn't understand by now that of which I'm capable. He's been punished in the past. For a time I thought he had learned his lesson. No, Vince, I regret to say it, but he's just a dimwit."

"That's too bad", Vince said sadly, "but I'm afraid you still haven't answered my question. What reason would I have for stepping into this position? To put it crudely, what's in it for me?"

"What's to your advantage? Vince, what do you have now? In your work as a Bounty Hunter you risk your life for others, and for pennies. You have gained a certain reputation among your associates, but has that brought you any more money? Is this a future for a Prince of the House of Este?

"Also, you must bear in mind that I bought the Ingle and the Buono land out of my own pocket. They will be yours to sell if you so wish."

"You call me a Prince?"

"Yes, that is a common term used by the Royal families for any son of the house of that family."

"That sounds funny! So I'm a Prince of the House of Este. It takes some getting used to."

I went to my safe and took out a few large envelopes. As I was doing this he said something about making big money on a few drug dealer raids, but when I asked him what he meant, he didn't repeat it, but smiled sheepishly. I think he regretted bringing that up.

The first envelope I showed him had a list of all the property owned by the family, and I could see that he could not help but be impressed. He didn't see all of this on our trip. I explained that during my watch I added the Fusco, Ingle and Buono lands, and that the latter two lands were still in my name.

I also told him I took the Neunkirken castle and land away from the rebellious d'Este family in Austria. I brought him up to date on the disposition of all the property. He had no idea it was so extensive.

He said, "You mean you raided the Castello, Uncle?"

"Yes. It had to be done. They were involved in criminal activities."

"Can you tell me what they were?"

"Cheating on our lumber operation and the son was dealing in drugs big time."

Vince leaned back in his chair and laughed heartily. When he got control of himself he said, "I guess it runs in the family."

"Would you please explain that?" I asked, feeling annoyed. I don't like flippancy.

"Perhaps later on, Uncle. Please be patient with me. It seems we have one thing in common." And then he laughed again.

I thought his behavior was a little strange, but I let it go and got back to business. I explained the red marks showing that the compound on Lipari had been sold, the summerhouse in Ventimiglia, the Boiardo building, and also the palazzo in Milano.

"Uncle, didn't you say you were not permitted to sell property under the old contract?"

"Yes! Vincenti used HIS privilege to sell the first three and I twisted his arm to sell the last one. That was the one he wanted to live in year round. I made sure he could no longer do it."

"I see! What's in the other envelopes?"

"This one shows the bank balance. I handed it over for him to read, and his eyes almost bugged out of his head.

"Eighteen million in U.S. dollars? And this is just the money in the bank?"

"Those figures are not up to the minute. "Terzo", (referring to my second son, Antonino the third) has used close to two million reconstructing the old castle at Neunkirken. He's made it into a sprawling villa and re-named it 'The Villa Laura', after his mother."

"Two million dollars? No wonder it looks so great. For that kind of money it should rival the Taj Mahal."

"Not Quite! It's nice, and he'll have to pay the money back in time, as the property continues to earn money. He'll make it work. You can have those figures if you want them."

"No, that won't be necessary! You have one more envelope there."

"Yes, this is a copy of the original contract I had to sign when I ascended to the title. Take these three envelopes home with you and study them. I want you to be familiar with what's in them. You must be conversant with all this for the day when you ascend to the title yourself."

"How can you make the decision when I haven't agreed to it yet?" Vince asked.

"Don't forget who you are, Vince. You're a Prince of the House of Este, as I said, and I as your Lord can order you to accept your fate."

"All right! I'll accept the fact that you can order it, but you must accept the fact that I'll make the final decision."

I laughed and said, "See? Was I wrong in considering you for the succession? You are feisty! Just what the family needs over there."

Then I got serious. "Vince, believe me, I'm tired."

I took a photo album off my bookshelf and said, "Look at the family. It's for these, your relatives, that you must do this work. They are too close to everything, and will not be able to make the hard decisions. It will take the fresh ideas of new blood and new eyes to continue the work and maintain the duchy."

"Duchy?"

"It's not legally a duchy, but it's certainly large enough to be one." I could see that my nephew was not thrilled by the idea that his whole life would change and he would be in another country. Well, that happened to me, and I survived. I added, "At the moment, I can see no other way."

He shook his head slowly and said, "This boggles my mind!"

"Vince, on your way home give some serous thought to your responsibilities. Talk it over with your parents and any of your siblings and other relatives. Do not discuss this with your rowdy friends and your paramours. This is family business."

"Uncle, I will think it over and discuss it with the family, but I don't relish the idea of being in that huge

Castello with people I don't know. I'll feel like I'm all alone."

"Don't worry! While you're thinking about all this, I'll be looking for a proper wife for you. That will take care of your loneliness." I laughed as I saw the shock of disbelief on his face.

There was a lot my nephew was not aware of, and one was the fact that my marriage to the Duchess Laura was also arranged. At the time I resisted the marriage with everything I had, and now I find myself in the position of seeing to it that my nephew was properly married in the same way.

There was a difference, however. In my time, I was in love with another, Marilyn Maiberg.

My nephew does not have that problem. I realized I had to learn as much about him as he did about me, so I got an idea. "Vince, I'm sure you kept a journal of all your activities working as a Bounty Hunter, is that not so?"

"Yes. I have to keep clear records in case I'm ever asked to testify in any of my cases. Why do you ask?"

"I want to read all those notes. Send them to me."

He sensed what I was after. "I'll do better than that. I'll bring them to you when I come to Florida again. Will that suit you?"

"Why, yes indeed. Do you like Florida?"

"It isn't that" he answered. "I just feel that I'd better get closer to you if we are going to understand each other, and make the proper decisions. I know you're a great man, and that I can learn from you, but I have to learn at your knee, so to speak. I won't get it right if I listen to others."

"Good thinking. I would have given a king's ransom to have heard one of my own sons say that."

Vince looked at me, and a sad expression came over his face. "It's been hard for you, hasn't it?"

"Well, I did take the blows, but even with all the mistakes I made, I think I can say that my wife loved me and benefited from my efforts. It's true it wasn't easy, but I can assure you that you will never have to face similar challenges."

After a pause he added, "Just the new ones!" he said, smiling broadly.

I told him of one little problem that had come up recently. "Some Lazzaroni in Bergamo have started extorting tribute from the manager of the Buono land. They said they would guarantee that our wheat fields will not burn if we pay a tribute."

"Why not get rid of them?"

"It's a small amount. Just continue paying them. Getting rid of them would invite too much trouble."

He shook his head. "I don't like that!"

"Live with it! It's nothing!
"

"Uncle, you have been living here, and you say Vincenti has been neglecting his duties. Who has taken care of the daily matters at the Castello?"

"My daughter Leonora has been running the household and keeping me informed."

Vince picked up the album again. He studied the photographs but even though he had met the family he asked, "Which one is Leonora?"

When I showed him he said nothing but looked at her image for a long time. As he stared at her picture, I said, "She is your first cousin, Vince"

He looked up at me quickly and said, "Oh, yes, of course! This is an old picture. She looks different now."

I didn't realize it, but his admiration was a hint of things to come.

Chapter Three

The Reluctant Duke

My brother Piero, Vince's father, called me and said that Vince was not happy with the situation. "He doesn't see the value of the opportunity you're offering him." Piero said. "We've been trying to tell him that he would be well off for the rest of his life, but he's making himself miserable. Doesn't this sound like déjà-vu to you?"

"Indeed it does. That's why I sympathize with him, but what am I to do?"

"He'll come around! Just give him time."

"I hope I have the time." I said

"Don't talk that way, Antonino. You're as healthy as a horse."

"Yeah! An old nag!"

After several months, Vince arrived at my villa in Florida for the second time and he brought with him a huge pile of papers. They were his Hunter journals. He also returned the envelopes I had given him.

"All this paper work! You've been a busy boy!"

"It's probably too detailed for your reading taste, but I didn't want to leave anything out. The law will be served"

"That will be fine. I have plenty of time to do what I want to do with all this..."

"And what is that?"

"Well, you know I've been writing about the family, and you are family, so I think I'll write a book about your adventures."

"Please don't think of it. I don't want the bad guys to get a line on me. Something like that will blow my cover. It will ruin my chances of getting more work as well as putting me in the danger of having my enemies retaliate against me. It's important that I remain anonymous."

"Don't give a thought to any enemies. Remember that they are stupid and wouldn't know how to take you even if they knew where you could be found. They would not want to run into you again.

"As far as earning money, your worries are over. I'm giving you a handsome allowance so that you don't have to do any more of that dangerous work. You must stay healthy if you are to be the next Duke."

"You mean you want me to sit around and do nothing?"

"Play tennis!"

"That's all? I can't do that all day."

"You've got your playmates. Oh yes, I know about them, you naughty boy!" We both laughed at that.

"I don't like being idle."

"For now, go for a swim in the pool. I want to start reading your journals. Don't tell anyone about who I am. They have no idea, and I don't want them to know."

I didn't have a private pool, so Vince went to the clubhouse pool where he could talk to all the geriatric people that live in these villas. No doubt they will be telling him of all their aches and pains, which is the main topic of their conversation. The secondary topic is the restaurants they like to go to.

I started speed-reading Vince's journals, and soon came across the stories about the raids on the drug banks that he laughed about. I understood what he meant about us having something in common, and had to laugh myself. "Pari siamo!" I said aloud. (We are the same!)

It was then that I decided that this would make an interesting book. There certainly was enough material there. I didn't quite understand why he wrote about the drug raids with such clarity. After all, they weren't legal raids, and he wouldn't want anyone asking questions, yet it was all here in every troubling detail.

When Vince got back to the house he was already starting to turn pink from the effects of lying in the sun. I should have warned him that the Florida sun is strong, and that he had to take it in easy steps. "I hope the sun didn't burn you." I said.

"I feel all right. I don't burn easily." he said, but he should have taken my precautionary advice. In a few days of sunning himself, he got sun poisoning and wound up in bed.

"Look at this, Uncle. My legs are swollen and feel stiff, and the skin feels like leather."

I had a doctor come, but he only prescribed a skin lotion. "He just has to rest, and the condition will take care of itself." the doctor said.

My nephew was not one to lie in bed, however, and as soon as he felt a little better he began moving around. He stayed out of the sun, thought. He learned that lesson.

One day he asked, "Uncle, I hope you'll excuse my impertinence, but why are you living in a place like this? I would think you'd be better off in the Castello degli Estensi rather than here."

"The sudden loss of Duchess Laura hit me very hard, and I could not stay in the Castello, knowing that her frail form lay in a coffin in the crypt below the chapel.

"I thought I could recover if I went back to my old haunts in New York City, but that didn't work. The city had changed too much, and I was no longer able to take the noise and dirt. The streets seemed to be full of weirdoes, and so I decided that retirement here would be best for me.

"It has proven so", I continued. " It's quiet here, and the place is kept clean. I can finish my days here, but I must be sure of the succession. That is first in my heart. The family must be taken care of and the Castello as well, so that my wife, in her eternal rest will lie undisturbed."

My nephew was looking at me intently, as if trying to study my very soul. Then he nodded, as if to say he saw what was there and agreed with it. "What about YOUR eternal rest? What would you like?"

"I'll die here, but I have the pedestal next to Laura's in the crypt. Have my coffin placed there."

"Consider it done, whether I become Duke or not."

"Vince, you must be the next Duke. I will not rest in peace knowing that some incompetent is in charge."

"Uncle, you make a compelling argument, but I'm still not sure I want this, and I'm reluctant to leave my life in New York,"

"Think ahead, Vince. What will your life be in, say ten years? Will you still want your present life then?"

"Good point!"

Vince stayed with me for two weeks but essentially our second round of conversations was over, and when he returned to New York, I busied myself with the new book which I entitled "Secrets of a Bounty Hunter" (It has been published by Lulu Publishers. Readers who are interested may order it from them at Lulu.com)

I didn't hear from my nephew for several months, but I didn't want to press him. He understood what was expected of him and he most certainly had been thinking about it. Would he "run for the border" as I did?

His father called a few times to ask certain questions about some details, and how the contract was to be worded and I assumed he was talking to Vince about it.

Naturally I answered his questions, understanding his own concern, and then said. "Let him take his time. There's no hurry, I hope."

Chapter Four

A letter arrives.

Again, several months went by and just as I began thinking that Vince was hoping the whole business would go away, I received a letter from him. He was going to prove to be a prolific writer.

Your Grace, my dear uncle,

As you wished, I have been thinking about your proposal, and also talking to the family, and I've decided, as a first step, to go to Italy and take a look at the present situation for myself.

I'll be honest. I'll be looking for any traps that I may be walking into. It's just my precautionary instincts kicking in. I'll be asking pointed questions to all the people involved, and I don't think they'll mind getting the third degree.

With your permission, I'll start for Italy in about a week's time. I'll give you an exact date when I know, and it will give you time to make whatever preparations you deem necessary.

With respect and affection, I am,
Your nephew, Vince

I had to smile first at his formality, then at his intention of giving my children and others "the third degree". This is going to be fun. My children will surely give HIM the third degree. He will soon see that although they are living a laid-back lifestyle, they are accustomed to discussing every point endlessly. They'll wear him out.

Not wishing to write letters, I called him one night and told him to pack for a long stay. "Everything takes time, Vince. You can't hurry the Italians. I had to learn that. It took me a long while to realize that they keep to their own timetable, and are confused by Americans who want to hurry everything."

"Don't worry, Uncle, I know how to get people to move their asses when they show a reluctance to do so."

"Now Vince, don't be hasty! Take a few months to get the feel of the place and try to get in with the right tempo. Don't make the mistakes I did. I was difficult and hot under the collar, and it took many years to overcome the fear and confusion I caused in the family."

"They have to learn about me too, don't they?"

"Exactly, so give them the time to do it. Remember, you're the interloper, so to speak. They'll need time to get used to the new situation.'

"Are they THAT fragile?"

"In a way, yes. You're coming into THIER home, and they don't know what to expect. Don't create the wrong impression. They are all good people. They are gentle people. Treat them as such."

"You're concerned that I'll be too rough?"

"Your life as a Bounty Hunter demonstrates that! Leave your handcuffs at home."

I heard him laughing at the other end. Then he said "Uncle, I have had some training at my mother's knee. I'm not like the proverbial bull in a china shop. I can be quite gentle and civil."

"That's my boy! Remember your manners at all times. Pardon me for being trite, but you get more cooperation with honey that you will with vinegar."

"Leave it to me. I'll spread the honey, most of the time."

"And why not ALL of the time?"

"Vincenti may need a little taste of vinegar. I don't trust him!"

"Vince, he's not a bad boy. Stupid, but not bad."

"Any suggestions on how I might deal with him?"

"For the present, leave him on the Fusco property. See what happens."

"I don't want him that close to me"

"Do you think he'll try to hurt you?"

"Is there a guarantee he won't try? He may not want to do the work, but he can still be resentful, feeling he's the proper heir."

"He made his bed, and now he must lie in it. If he thinks he's the rightful Duke, step on him!"

"Thank you! That's what I had to hear."

Chapter Five

A second letter

While I am in semi-retirement in Florida, I can only report on my nephew's activities and thoughts from either his letters or the communication of others, meaning generally hearsay, or those times when I spoke directly to him on the phone.

As I am writing this book, I could see that it was going to be difficult to convince him to step into the duties I had in mind for him. He was not showing any haste in coming to a decision, and I could only wait.

Well, I was busy on the Bounty Hunter book, and I was also busy making inquiries about a wife for this reluctant young man. Once the word got around in Italy, the offers started coming in. I was not too impressed with any of them, but then one day word came from the father of a college girl, who said he was a relative of the Duchess Laura.

"Nice to hear from you, but tell me, what can I do for you?

"I have a marriageable daughter, Gilda, who is studying at the University of Bologna," he said simply. Then he added he was a second cousin, and I was surprised that I had never heard of him. I said I'd call him back and took down his phone number.

Before we hung up I asked. "You say your daughter is studying at the University in Bologna? That's where my daughter Beatrice is a professoressa, and is teaching languages and math. I'll call you back soon, Senor Colonna and will let you know if I'm interested."

"Thank you, Your Grace".

I checked with my mother-in-law, and it proved that he was indeed a relative of the Colonna family. She said, "He visited the Castello while you were in the hospital, to pay his respects, and he left when he heard you were going to be all right."

"Was his wife and daughter there?"

"No they weren't, but they did send their respects."

"Thank you, mother! What do you think?"

"I have no opinion, not knowing enough about Gilda or Vince. I'll wait and observe before I'll venture my own thoughts on all of this."

Well! The old girl has mellowed completely!

I had Beatrice check on Gilda, and she reported that the girl was a bright student, and very nice looking.

There was also some royalty in the family's background of course, being a Colonna, so the idea became more favorable by the day. I spoke to the girl's father again, and said that I was interested in pursuing the matter. He seemed very happy at the prospect.

I asked him if his daughter had been told, but he said she hadn't, but that he would remedy that now that I was interested. He asked for a brief description of Vince.

I wasn't going to sugarcoat the pill. "He's a tough man, who has been making his living as a Bounty Hunter, but he's from a good family, being my brother's son, and he's a talented tennis player, having won the New York State Championship a few years ago. He shows good manners and is very intelligent."

"My daughter is a sweet and gentle person. Do you think there will be a good match between them?"

"One never can know such things, but I can only say he impresses me and I think he'll be a good protector and provider."

"Thank you, Your Grace. I'm sure we'll know more after they meet."

There the matter rested for a while, but when my brother told his son Vince that a wife was found for him, he turned white. He finally called me and complained that I certainly did not waste any time. I laughed at that, but he was clearly nonplussed.

"Uncle, suppose I don't like her, or she doesn't want me. Have you thought of that"?

I said, "I don't have to worry about such things. Go to Italy and meet her!" I heard a moan at the other end of the line and I said, "Oh, come on you big baby! Are you afraid of one little college girl?"

"Not a little college girl, but if she wants to be my wife, then I'm damned scared! Uncle, can you cut me some slack for a while?"

"You've had enough time and enough slack. Jump into the pool and get wet. You're not doing anything important, so get on a plane and get over there!"

He said meekly, "All right. Talk to you later."

A letter came from Vince some time later. It showed that he was already getting into the Italian way of doing things; He probably had some advice from someone in the Castello, most probably Leonora.

Your Grace,
    I arrived at the airport in Milano in good order and was whisked to the Castello in good time. Everyone has treated me most kindly, but they are so reserved that I do not know if they are happy to welcome me to the life here.

    I have explained to them that I was uncertain about everything, and that the last thing I wanted to do was make anyone unhappy. They seemed to appreciate that.
    There was a family gathering and I met a lot of people. How big is this family anyway? I remember the mob scene when I came to Italy with you the last time, when you got so sick. There are a lot of people ready to pay you homage.
    I didn't know who was who then, but now I realize that most of them that came to see you were actually family. That's astounding! Will I be in charge of all of THEM, and be responsible for their welfare? It will be more like running a small government. What are you getting me into?
    The only ones not present were Cousin Beatrice and Cousin Isabella. Of course Isabella has a good

reason, but Beatrice could have been among the greeters.

They have a way of doing everything that seems to suggest that they are going to live forever. They neither hurry nor get excited over anything.

Meanwhile I'm as nervous as a cat. I am to meet Gilda this afternoon at her house. Leonora will come with me. I'm sure glad I don't have to go there alone.

Right now I hope her family will like me. I have given no thought as to whether I will like her. In fact, I have not given any thought about anything. My mind is in suspended animation.

Dear Uncle, Are you sure we're doing the right thing? It all seem so bizarre to me.

Respectfully, Your nephew, Vince

When I read the letter to his father over the phone, we both laughed uproariously. "What a nervous Nellie!" his father said.

"He'll be fine!" I said, "New situations always seem a little bizarre. We'll hear about his visit to the Colonnas. That should be good for another laugh."

I called di Dante, the family secretary at the Castello and asked for Vince, but he said my nephew was out in the field jogging. (Note: Conversation is in Italian but translated for my American readers.)

"He's been doing that every day, Your Grace. Why does he do it?" the secretary asked.

"He's a tennis player, and he does it to keep fit."

"Well, the foreman told me that the field workers think it a strange apparition. They think he's out of his mind, expending his energy that way."

"Tell the foreman he'll be the next Duke, and he's not as crazy as they may think."

"Yes, Your Grace, I did tell him that, but I don't think the workers are comfortable with the idea that the new Duke is out of his mind."

"Well, my nephew will find it hard to live down that first impression. Please have him call me when he gets back."

"Yes, Your Grace."

I thought I made a fine choice in both the new Duke and his new Duchess. Yes, the family will be all right with those two.

When the call came in from Vince he sounded like he was out of breath. "Is everything all right, Uncle?"

"Yes, everything is fine. I received your letter, and I called to assure you that we are doing the right thing. Vince, can you stop worrying over nothing? Just relax and get comfortable with the new life and the new ways. You'll find that you're being accepted, even thought they seem cool to you. They are a reserved people but they'll warm up to you soon enough."

"I hope you're right! I'm feeling more like a stranger in paradise every day."

"Don't be so dramatic. Trust what I tell you, and for

Heaven's sake, trust yourself, too."

"What do you mean?"

"Don't be afraid to tell them what you want. Give orders! You'll see how they jump when you speak. Tell them what you want for dinner. Tell them you want your rooms cleaned. Anything, but show them that you're in command. They will feel more secure if you show them you're the Duke."

"Uncle, are you serious? I'm not the new Duke. Won't they object if I start flexing my muscles?"

"Can't you see that that's exactly what they expect and need? The job requires new thinking on your part. Get into it!"

"All right, I'll try it, but I feel an impending disaster coming my way. I think I'm afraid of them."

"Don't show fear or doubt. Then they will be contemptuous of you. Stand firmly on your feet, but don't be unreasonable. The one thing they expect first of all is fairness."

"I'm afraid I'll be calling you every day of the week."

"Don't be silly! You've got Marco di Dante, the secretary, there to help you. And his wife Aurelia has been teaching there, so she knows the youngsters as well as the staff. Don't rely on the Countess Colonna. She'll take some getting used to. Good luck with HER!"

"Oh, boy! I'm in the soup!"

"No you're not! All right! Enough of this! Get with the program, or you WILL be in the soup before long. Talk to you later." When I hung up I had to smile at the humor of the situation. He could catch criminals and go on drug raids, but he's cowed by a bunch of people who don't know how to be brave. He'll learn. Will he ever learn!

He began first by asking question, and they were simple enough to answer. Questions like "What do you do? Where are your quarters? How do you like it here? And so forth.

Then the questions started getting harder to answer. Vince was going around asking everyone, including the staff, what they would like to see in the way of changes.

This brought the Countess Colonna out of her cocoon and she started to coach Vince about the separation of the Aristocracy and commoners. "The staff has no opinions about what should change here. Blah, blah blah," and so on, ad infinitum!"

The other members of the family chimed in and before Vince knew it every one was jabbering away about something, He had created a Frankenstein with his questions. When I heard about it I had to sit down, the laughter was shaking me so much.

Welcome to Italy, Vince!

Chapter Six

A quick fight.

The family secretary, Marco di Dante, called me and said, "Your Grace, I'll give you the good news first, then the bad news. When Michele drove your nephew to Gilda Colonna's house, her parents were there but she was not.

"After chatting with them for a while, he found them easy to get along with, and then he decided to be driven to the University, the idea being to visit both his cousin, your daughter Beatrice, and to see Gilda. That's the good news. Now for the bad news!

"When they arrived at the University parking lot, Michele saw a space and started to pull into it when a young man on a motor scooter cut them off and pulled in ahead of them.

"As I understand the event, the young man got off the scooter then laughed at them and flipped them the finger. Vince jumped out of the limo and started pushing the scooter into some bushes to clear the parking spot, when the young man swung the belt holding his books and hit Vince in the back...

"He had his books tied together with this leather belt, and as your nephew continued to dump the scooter into the bushes, the young man started swing his books again. That's when your nephew stepped in and punched him, but good!

"According to Michele, blood squirted out of the man's face and he went down. There were no witness to the incident besides Michele, but soon there was a crowd of students forming a circle, and someone had called an ambulance.

"The ambulance arrived, and the police with it. They wanted to arrest your nephew, but Michele identified himself as a former policeman, and when the police heard the story, they did not make the arrest.

"Vince decided to go to the hospital with the man, who turned out to be a student at the University. At the hospital, the doctors found that the student had a broken nose and serious cracks around the left eye socket. They could not believe that a fist did all that damage.

"They were convinced when x-rays showed that two of Vince's knuckles had been pushed out of place, and they saw a crack in the third metatarsal bone. The hand had to be re-set and put in a cast.

"The parents of the student arrived at the hospital and at first wanted to press charges, but they were also dissuaded when they learned the facts, and the person who did the damage was to be the next Duke. Your Grace, it seems you have quite a reputation around these parts.

"Your daughter Beatrice is angry and ashamed that the incident took place on the University campus. She has taken some time off and is going to stay at the Castello for a few days.

Gilda said she refuses to marry such a rough man, referring to him as a barbarian. It was fortunate that Vince told Leonora not to come on the trip. She would have been witness to this carnage.

"Your Grace, in my humble opinion, you have chosen the right man for the next Duke. He has the strength of ten!

There will be no doubts in anyone's mind that he will cut a wide swath."

I thanked di Dante for his report, and could not wait to call Vince's father. He said that this called for a celebration. "We have a new Duke!"

I told him to go ahead and celebrate, but as for me, I just wanted to rest on my laurels. I was feeling mighty smug!

The next day I got a call from my baby, Leonora. She told me that Beatrice was livid over Vince's behavior and the Gilda has decided she will not marry him and wants nothing to do with him.

"Well", she continued, "he's all right in my book! When he got home I greeted him with a big hug and kissed him on both cheeks. No one is going to mess with our Vince!"

OUR VINCE! Before we hung up the phone, I asked Leonora if she would find out if OUR VINCE would deign to call his Duke, and then sat back and breathed a long sigh of satisfaction. I could not have made a better choice. Now, will he pick up the standard and run with it? I was still not sure he would. Good Heavens! What else could I offer him? He'll be getting EVERYTHING!

Leonora did not tell me everything. When my nephew called he told me he was ashamed of himself. "I should have restrained myself, realizing that he was only a smart-assed student, and that Italian men are given too much bravura, especially the young ones."

"Don't' worry too much about him. His sort are a dime a dozen."

"Well, I could have thought of myself, too."

"What do you mean?"

"My right hand is all wrapped up. The doctor had to pull my knuckles back into place and now I have to wear a cast on my right hand. Only my thumb and pinky are sticking out. It hurts like the very devil."

"You've knock men out before. Why was this any different?"

"All I thought of was hitting him with all I had, and I guess I did. He'll need several operations to re-construct his bones, and his face will never be the same. His pretty-boy days are over."

"He won't lack for romance, there are many women who think ugliness is handsome, and will flock around him. Give him time, and he'll come up with a story of bravery beyond the call of duty. The girls will swoon."

"I don't know about that, Uncle. I hope you're right for his sake. I'd hate the think I ruined his life. When I saw him in the hospital, part of his face was caved in. The doctors did not believe I just punched him with my fist. They agreed that no fist could do that much damage until they examined my hand."

Get their names, I'll send them a copy of the book I'm basing your adventures on as a Bounty Hunter. They'll be convinced."

He laughed, and then said. "It was a bad thing all around."

"It's the making of your reputation. You have no idea how the news of this will get around. Anyone who might think of giving you trouble will change his mind when they think of their own faces." I had to laugh at my own words.

"You're taking this very lightly, uncle. I'm deeply troubled by it. Gilda won't even talk to me, and I haven't met her yet."

"Give her a chance to think about it. I thought you understood women. The more she thinks about your savagery, the more she'll find you attractive. Did any of your New York lovelies shrink from you?"

"Well, uncle, I didn't tell them what I did for a living, and for that very reason."

"Years ago there was a very pretty Norwegian girl, a popular ice skater named Sonja Heinie, a real, clean northern European beauty! She was in several movies and I'm sure most men who saw her would have loved to marry her.

She had a torrid affair with one of the ugliest black men you'll ever see, a prizefighter named Joe Louis. He looked like a gorilla and he could hardly put two words together to make a sentence. He was that stupid!"

"Your point being?"

"No one can predict what a woman will go for. Some women go for the worst kind, the more brutal the better. Miss Heinie passed up the most handsome actors in Hollywood, and went for King Kong, an illiterate ape"

"Somehow your words aren't helping, uncle."

"How did Leonora greet you when you came home?"

"She surprised me with her affection. She had been so reserved before that."

"See?"

"Oh, yes, well, so you think Gilda will come around?"

"I guarantee it. In fact I'll bet on it."

"No thanks, uncle. You have a magical way of being right! OK, I'll just let her think things over, and see what happens."

"She'll fall into your arms!" I laughed again and we agreed to talk soon again.

A short time later, Count Giulio Villano called and wanted to discuss the news about the new hero. He was his usual ebullient self and said that he was helping to spread the word about the new Saint George in our midst.

I laughed and told him not to exaggerate the story, or Vince will have many ladies in distress calling on him.

"I shouldn't doubt it", Villano said. "He's certainly handsome enough."

"What you can do Giulio, is to find him a tennis club. He'll want to play, and he'll need good opponents. We have to keep the man happy."

"I'll get right on it! Oh, by the way, I have some information on those extortionists in Bergamo. There are five of them, and they hang out in a men's club. It's just a small store. Ciao!"

Good old Count Villano. I continue to rely on him, and he's always there for the family and me. Drat! I forgot to ask about Lucrezia and Damiano. I guess they're all right, or I would have heard something.

I also forgot about Vince's hand. How was he going to play tennis with a busted hand?

Chapter Seven

Fact finding

Vince wrote:

Dear, Uncle,

My visit to the Fusco Manor held many surprises. I expected to find a resentful Vincenti and a docile Regina, but it proved to be the other way around.

Vincenti, upon letting me in the door, looked at my broken hand and spoke very respectfully. I was seated in the salon, and soon Regina came in followed by a maid who had a tray with coffee and snacks.

I told Vincenti that I was not going to waste any time on polite conversation and that I was much aggrieved that he proved to be wanting when it came time for him to step up to the plate and assume the ducal responsibilities.

He was left with no doubt in his mind that I did not regard him as a viable family member, and that because of him I was being pressed into the family service.

Vincenti was docile all the while, but it was Regina who began shouting at me. "How do you think *I* feel? I was told I was to marry the Duke and become the Duchess of the Castello. Now I'm being treated as an outcast."

I explained to Regina that it was nothing of my doing, but that when I AM named to the succession, they both will be sent to Uruguay.

At this Regina began to cry. She was inconsolable for a time and I waited until she stopped her wailing, and then said that I didn't think life in Uruguay would be too harsh.

She said I was being unfair, but I told her that she was ready and willing to live the life of luxury and ease in Milano, never encouraging her husband to do his duty. "You are just as culpable as he," I said. "Did you both think you were going to get away with that and neglect the family? You took the word PRIVILEGE to heart didn't you? And with no thought as to what the rest of the family needed."

"We didn't KNOW!"

"That may have been true at the outset, but you did nothing even after you were warned!"

"Well, we didn't take that seriously!" she cried. The tears started flowing again. All the while Vincenti just sat there, allowing his wife to get upset. Then she pleaded, "What about our baby?"

"Where were you, in Limbo? Did you really entertain the notion that the Duke was going to stand by and watch the land he worked so hard for go to seed? I'm sorry, but the die is cast! There's nothing I can do! Your baby will have to accept the fate you both have designed for it."

"We can live here! My husband is doing a good job here!"

"Will you try to UNDERSTAND? I will NOT have Vincenti at my back. Do you take me for a fool?"

"He will give you his solemn word he will not do anything to harm or denigrate you, won't you Vincenti?"

He seemed to rouse himself from a dream when he heard his name. "What?"

Uncle, I'm convinced you can never rely on Vincenti. There's something wrong with him. I can think of no solution for them other than to send them to Uruguay where they will be under the watchful eye of the Count Cesare.

Respectfully, Vince

This letter saddened me. Vince is most adamant where it comes to Vincenti, and I too cannot think of what to do with them. Is it hopeless?

It was not! Some days later, another letter came from Vince. This time he was in Neunkirchen and talking to Antonino "Terzo" d'Este. He had already told me what he had in mind for "Terzo", and I didn't expect anything new in this letter. I was surprised!

Dear Uncle,

I had arrived at the Villa Laura expecting to read Terzo the riot act concerning his spending, but when I told him of my visit to Vincent and Regina at the Fusco Manor, he solved all of our problems with three little words.
He said, "I'll take them!"
I blush to admit that I didn't think of that solution myself. Of course there's a catch to it, as we might expect from the sly "Terzo"
He said, "Of course you understand that I'll have to build them an attachment to the Villa, and that will take money!"
I suspect that if we leave Terzo to his own devices, he'll find a way to drain every cent out of the bank. I'm exaggerating, of course, and I must admit that he does use the money to good purposes, but how much leeway are you willing to give him?
I have the feeling that he thinks the money is coming from a bottomless pit.

Your nephew, Vince

I also liked what Terzo was doing with the money but I had to agree that he couldn't continue to spend at such an alarming rate. What I didn't understand was why Terzo felt he had to build an addition to the main building. He has several suites on the second floor, any one of which could accommodate Vincenti, Regina and the coming baby. I decided to send a letter to Vince, with a copy to Terzo.

Vince,

I heartily approve of Terzo's offer to take Vincenti and Regina in with him at the Villa Laura. What I do not approve of is his desire to build the addition to the villa to accommodate them. Such an addition is unnecessary. They can choose one of the suites on the second floor, one with an extra room for the baby when it arrives, and which would accommodate a maid.

Terzo will have to start economizing. The renovations he's been making there should be finished by now. He must stop making changes all the time, and be satisfied with what he's got.

He should be grateful that I originally approved his plans, and appreciate that both my generosity and my patience are just about at an end.

Uncle Antonino

Vince was back at the Castello degli Estensi when my letter arrived, and I understand he talked to Terzo, and my second son was disappointed and did not want to take Vincenti into the Villa anymore.

I called Terzo and asked him why he changed his mind. He said, "I don't mind taking my brother and his wife into the villa, but I don't want him living right in the main house. If he's always inside the main building he will cause trouble, but if he's in a separate apartment, he'll have less excuse to stick his nose in where it doesn't belong."

"You've got a good point there. All right, find out what such a structure will cost, and send me the plans."

"Thank you, father! I knew you'd understand. I think you'll agree also that Vincenti will have to work. There's no room for dead wood in this place. I'm not running a charity."

"Neither am I, Terzo! Please bear that in mind. Just tell Vincenti that although you're his younger brother, YOU are in charge at the Villa Laura, and that he is to cooperate with you, or it's Uruguay for him."

"I most certainly will! If he shirks or causes trouble I'll ship him to Uruguay."

"Good enough!"

"By the way, father, I have another plan, and I hope you see the practicality of this as well. I want to build a cabin in the woods for some of the lumbermen to stay in overnight. Their presence in the forest will discourage poachers. How does that sound to you?"

"How much will THAT cost?"

"I won't need any money for that. It will just be a simple affair, and I can get the material from what's lying around in the work yard."

"OK, that's a plan I can live with!"

I then sent a letter to the Fusco Manor House:

Vincenti and Regina,

There has been a new development, and you may not have to go to Uruguay after all. Your brother Terzo has agreed to take you into his villa at Neunkirchen, but you'll have to stay at the Fusco Manor until the apartment he will build for you is ready.

If the plans show that the apartment is commodious, you and the baby can move there. Vincenti, you will be expected to work. You must give me your word that you will follow your brother's lead and not cause any problems for him or his workers.

You must consider this to be your last chance. Terzo is under no obligation to put up with any of your nonsense. Be good and tend to your work, and your child will have a chance to grow up in a good environment.

Whatever you do, never rile up your cousin Vince. He has a hair-trigger temper, and will surly break your bones if you step out of line. You've already seen him in action, so mind yourself, and take care of your family.

Go with my blessings,
Your father.

Chapter Eight

Another fight

After the incident in the parking lot at the University of Bologna, my daughter Beatrice went back to the Castello, "for a few days" to let the whole matter cool off. She was still there after a week, so her man friend, one Francesco della Rovere, went there to see her.

He was a colleague of hers at the University, and taught science there. They had been dating steadily for some time, but as yet there had been no talk of an engagement or marriage.

During his visit he became fascinated with the appointments in the Crystal Room, and one morning Vince, broken hand and all, was preparing to go out for his morning jog and saw Francesco sitting in the throne chair.

His right hand was in a cast you'll recall, but that didn't deter him from expressing his objection. "Why are you sitting there?" he asked Francesco.

"Who are YOU to ask?"

Beatrice, who related this story was just entering the Crystal Room and saw Vince reach over with his left hand and grab Francesco by the throat.

When Beatrice called me to complain, she said, "He fairly lifted him out of the throne chair and I thought he would throttle the life out him right there and then. Father, Vince is a very dangerous man. How can you think of him for the succession?"

I told her to be patient. "Vince just has to settle down and learn our ways. Don't worry; he'll do very well for the family. I have every confidence in him."

"Francesco is leaving the Castello! Am I not to have any friends visiting me?"

Your friend was sitting in the throne chair. Think about that!"

"It was all so innocent. Why should he be treated like a criminal for that?

"Are you sure it was so innocent?"

"What are you alluding to?"

"Could he be a fortune hunter?"

"Oh no! Not Francesco! How could you even suggest it?"

"Have you ever seen Vince sitting in the ducal chair?"

"Well, no, but what does that signify?"

"It signifies that he shows the proper respect for the meaning of the throne chair, and apparently your friend does not."

"Well, Francesco is liberal minded. He regards such things as mere symbols of a by-gone age."

"And do YOU regard it as a symbol of a by-gone age?"

"No father. I remember when you sat in that chair, and I think of it, and you, fondly and respectfully."

"Well, now Francesco will think of it, and me, fondly and respectfully, too."

"Are you always going to side with Vince against your children?"

"You're being silly Beatrice, and you're forgetting your manners. Vince will be the new Duke. Make it your business to get on the right side of him."

"Yes, father but I don't like it. He's dangerous!"

"He is, but only to those who ask for trouble. Now be a good girl, and when you talk to your Francesco, remind him that when he visits the Castello to leave his liberal thinking back at that liberal rat's nest you call a university, because if he gets out of line Vince will throttle him for sure, and he has my leave to do it."

"All right father, but---"

"No buts, Beatrice! We are not having an intellectual discussion! Now do as you're told!"

My daughter Beatrice was always the cerebral one, and like so many eggheads, she sometime misses the overall point of life and its everyday meaning. I recall the story of the University professor, a man of genius, who was preparing to leave his house one day and saw that it was raining outside. He reached for his raincoat but the hesitated. He thought, "What if the raincoat has a hole in it?" Eggheads! Educated beyond their intelligence!

Vince is learning fast. I have to back him to the hilt if I am to keep him on the job. I feel that once he has settled in and is married, he will stay the course to the end.

The end! I can't see the end of MY work yet, so I can't predict his future for him, either. My need for Vince makes me wonder why my own children are so hopeless in seeing to the needs of their own environment.

I guess one can find examples of this in history, where the people who make their families wealthy cannot pass that expertise to their own children. Is this why great families fade away, or even how great nations do? It's so sad, but maybe there's a reason for this in the universal plan.

I fear the worst. Vince has called and said he must return to New York for medical treatment. He feels his hand is not healing well and does not trust Italian doctors to get it right. I could only give my approval and asked him to call me when he got there. He did.

"I just got back from seeing the doctor and he quickly took x-rays and told me that the bone setting was all right but needed some adjusting... I asked him why I was in such pain. After all, I had broken bones before and don't remember having this much agony. He said there might be a pinched nerve but assured me that everything was all right and gave me some pain-killers and made a date for minor surgery."

I asked him, "So, when are you going back to Italy?"

"Uncle, if it's all right with you I'd like to recover here. I've already been in two fights and I'll probably cause more trouble if I go back now. Are you all right with this?"

"Yes, of course. Take your time. You've already done a magnificent job, so you deserve a rest."

"What magnificent job? I made everybody angry, and I'm sure they're glad to see the last of me. Beatrice won't even look at me."

"No, and she'll get over it. I've read her the riot act. I'm with YOU, and so is Leonora. She's quite impressed with you, probably because she sees a little of me in you."

"How so?"

"You've shown them that you're not going to waste any time demonstrating who the boss is. That's the good part."

"And the bad part?"

"Remember I told you not to scare them! Use the honey approach when you return. They know you better now, so if you treat them sweetly, they will breath a sigh of relief and will learn to love you soon enough.

"Thanks, uncle. I'll call you soon again."

"Fine! Be ready to give me a detailed description of what happened over there."

"Didn't Michele tell you?"

"Yes, but I want to hear it in your own words." I couldn't help laughing.

"What's so amusing?"

"You are! Can't you see the funny side to all this?"

"Help me out!"

"You have that whole area of Italy talking, and you were only there a week!

"Have people been talking to you?"

"Just about everybody! You're a hit, Vince."

"I'm glad you think so! I'll call you tomorrow."

What Vince doesn't realize about the Italians is that they love to have something to talk about, and the topic of the new American Duke and his ferocity will make the rounds for some time to come.

I didn't meet Francesco della Rovere on my last trip to Italy and during my stay in the Castello degli Estensi. During my illness he did not show the courtesy or the respect to visit and meet me. Although I would like to see my daughter Beatrice married, I fault her too, for not having the presence of mind to see that I met him.

To make excuses, perhaps they were not serious about their relationship at the time, but since then I have heard that the relationship had taken a serious turn. The man has some good credentials, He is descended from one of the Montefeltro Dukes, but I don't remember which one.

It seems to me that this Francesco stands among the prissy intellectuals that the Universities in Italy are turning out today. Judging from the incident in the crystal room, he is not a fighter, but a puppy that readily tucks his tail between his legs and runs for cover.

I shall have to talk to Beatrice about that.

Vince called me again after a short time and informed me that he thought he was healing nicely, and would start thinking about his return to Italy. I thanked him for relieving my mind on that score, and asked if he had anything in the way of changes to be implemented in the business structure.

"Not in the family business as yet, since Marco seems to have everything down pat, so I'll confer with him before ranging around the properties. I do want to check on Terzo to see if he is keeping his new addition to the Villa Laura modest in its structure and use."

"Good thinking. Clap the reins on him."

"Yes, I can see that he continues to modify, and we have to be sure his modifications are worth the money, and that he's not chasing his tail."

"Not chasing his tail! I like that! So what are you doing to pass the time in New York City?

"Do you want me to give you the whole menu? Don't laugh, but I tried playing tennis lefty, and it was a source of merriment to my friends and other onlookers. My groundstrokes stink, but the funniest thing was trying to toss the ball up for the serve holding it daintily between my thumb and pinkie. Needless to say, the cast got in the way."

"What else have you been doing?"

"Uncle, I think you're driving at something. Yes, I did call my girl friend. We went out for the evening, and yes, she stayed to cool my fevered brow. There are some things the cast does NOT interfere with."

"Be careful! Gilda is mad at you, and if she gets word that you're bedding down one of your ladies, she'll never soften her opinion of you. She thinks you're a barbarian. Don't do anything to re-enforce that idea."

"Uncle, a man's got to eat!"

"Don't give me any of you city logic. You know damned well what I'm saying!"

He sounded contrite. "Yes, uncle, I'll be the very epitome of discretion."

Well, Vince wasn't perfect, but who is? He must learn to rein in that temper of his and mind his P's and Q's.

Chapter Nine

Vince's Father

Vince was going to need some minor surgical adjustments on his injured right hand, and after the treatment, intended to spend a few weeks at his parent's house even though he had his own apartment. He didn't want to try managing with only his left hand.

I welcomed this news because it will give him a chance to re-connect with his father, and thus I will get more information about his activities. I did not like his being alone in his apartment, and toying around with his playmates anyway.

There was the other matter of his associates. He worked with some questionable characters when he was active as a Bounty Hunter, and some of his friends were near criminal themselves, despite the fact that they stayed just inside of the legal line most of the time.

Running around and conferring with these people led him into some very borderline activities, and it's amazing he wasn't investigated himself. Nobody is interested now, but there was a time when those drug raids he was party to could have landed him in jail.

That's all the family needed; a Prince of the House of Este as a jailbird. Not that there wasn't some questions raised during my watch at the Castello degli Estensi. The Police were there several times for different reasons, one being the case of fratricide when his son murdered my neighbor, Count Fusco.

(See book "An American Duke in Italy", Lulu.com)

Nor am I raising any questions about Vince's character. It is his special qualities that he demonstrated as a Bounty Hunter that makes him so suitable for the job of Duke of the House of Este. Why? For the very reason that it is the lack of courage to fight that makes my own sons unfit. The job requires a person who will take the bit in his mouth and run with it.

Being the Duke, and overseeing the vast land and other holdings of the House of Este, requires boldness and a ready willingness to take on the troublemakers and meet them with force, when necessary.

This not only will discourage enemies, but also will give the family the sense of security they need to function and make the continual preparations for the future of the House.

Firstly, the family must act like the aristocrats they are, and the children must continually be educated so that the next generation and the next are clear on what it is that they must maintain.

Secondly, the fieldwork is almost constant, with a few short breaks during the year that helps the Contadini catch their breaths. These things require constant attention, and there's no room at the top for fops or for indolence of any sort.

This was the problem when I first went to the Castello. The denizens were living in a dream world that was about to collapse around their ears. There's no point in belaboring the reasons here. All this was explained in previous books.

The important point now is that the whole thing can come crashing down again without a strong man at the helm, and I think that Vince, despite his reluctance and his fiery temper, fills the bill.

Well, it isn't as though I have a choice. There's simply no one else. In fact, I'm lucky to have him, IF I have him, that is. The most unpleasant of my thoughts these critical days is that if I lose him, I will lose the duchy.

How can it be held together, and if it splits up, how can we maintain our strength and political muscle? It would be a sad loss to both the family and that whole section of the Italian peninsular, particularly the Emilia-Romagna region.

A break up is the last thing that the Monarchist Party wants to see too. The main objective of this political party is to recall and re-seat the Italian King on the throne. The Italian Aristocracy does not want to see its position weakened by anything.

While Vince is convalescing at his father's house, my brother Piero will explain all this to him in great detail. Of course I'll have my oar in those discussions since I know all about this situation first hand.

The operation on Vince's right hand was successful and he is now spending quality time with his father and mother. He's in pain and is wearing a long face, but with a little time and some good eating, he'll be his old self again.

One question is how long will he stay quiet without his "nookie"? Maybe his favorite squeeze can visit him and "chat" with the horny toad in his room.

I decided to ask him to come down to Florida to spend some time with me.

Good news came from Italy. Gilda has decided to reconsider her refusal to marry Vince. I cannot say whether her father talked to her, or whether as I told Vince, she is secretly thrilled at being married to a brute. Yes, there is something in the psyche of the female of the species that makes them more interested in the dominating male that they wish to have known.

That's all right. Let them have their little games. When a man is interested in a woman, he wants her to be interested in him no matter what her reasons may be. What does that matter, as long as he can get laid regularly?

Do you think that's cynical? Ask any woman why she is attracted to a particular man, and she will lie to you! Since we'll never get the truth from them, why should we care what their real reasons are? Maybe THEY don't know either!

The old saw says that it's a woman's prerogative to change her mind. Dare we ask, "What mind?" I don't mean to suggest that she doesn't have a mind, only that we don't know which mind she's using at any given moment.

Gilda is young, but she displays all the markings of the female mental changeability. They are born with it. It must serve some universal purpose. Who knows? The women themselves can't tell you, so what are we men to make of it?

Vince's father called me. "Antonino, when I told Vince that Gilda changed her mind and will marry him, he smiled an enigmatic smile that I cannot fathom. Did he ever indicate to you how he feels about Gilda? I hope he doesn't plan to give the poor girl a hard time."

"No, he never said anything to me, but I wouldn't worry about that. He treats all his girlfriends well, so he's not disposed to be hard on women. What I'd be concerned about is whether he takes women seriously. He doesn't seem to, and he'll have to learn that he has to listen to his wife."

Piero said, "If he doesn't take Gilda seriously now, he'll soon learn to. You know very well that when a woman becomes a wife, she comes equipped with all the tools needed to get and keep his attention."

I had to agree with that. "Yes, what was it that Dad called it? "The smell of the wick"! He has his own way of thinking about it." I heard Piero laughing.

"I wish I could remember all his quaint sayings, especially, the ones having to do with women. He could be very funny. What was that nickname he had for momma?"

"He used to call her 'Zinvadoza', but I have no idea what it means."

"Yeah, he had some great expressions. I'll keep you informed about our little neophyte. Right now he's miserable, but he'll be fine once he gets a taste of the wick!"

"Piero, give him some of the history of the family, and what it means for us to hold everything together in the present day. It has come to the point where even the neighbors and total strangers are depending on the stability of the House of Este."

"Antonino, what's worrying you? There doesn't seem to be any signs of deterioration. The family is holding together, and it will unless some outside danger threatens your little empire. What are you seeing that has you worried?"

"Listen Piero, I was the one that was there through all those bad times. I know how bad it was, and how easily it can become that way again. It's only by the showing of strength that we can hold the fort. Don't be fooled by the quiet and stable times we are experiencing now."

"Antonino, do you see any problems in the immediate future?"

"No, it's not that. I know only too well that if people begin to sense any kind of weakness, even our friends may move in to pick up any pieces they can. History shows that only too well, especially Italian history."

"I'm not arguing with you. I'm merely asking if you see anything coming. You seem to be expecting some catastrophe and I would like to know what is troubling you, that's all."

"Perhaps I'm being overly cautious, but my son's failures are bothering me, and I see it as a pattern for the future in just about all young Italian men. There is a strange lack of ambition and thought for the future. We must always have our eyes on the future, not only for our families, but the nation as well."

"You feel they can't see the importance of things?"

"Damn it, Piero, they just don't CARE! I don't know what the matter is, but Italian men don't care much about anything except arguing about everything. That's the national sport."

"I don't think you're going to be able to inspire the Italian men. They have a mindset that is pretty hardened, and they dare all comers to challenge their way of thinking."

"I think you're right, but we can change the rules!"

"What do you mean?"

"It's time we begin to think about women inheriting property and running things. The all-male macho thing is a tired cliché, and it's probably time to re-think the whole business. The men are too damned sure of themselves. That ought to knock them out of their lethargy."

"Such an idea will not be too well received. You don't want to pull down years of comfortable traditions."

"Why not? We do it here in America all the time. The Italian male needs a swift kick in the ass. Italy is becoming more and more of a second-class nation because of the lethargic way Italian men address real problems of the country. Consensus seems to be a dirty word in Italy."

Piero chuckled. "So women are going to save the day?"

"Who do you think has been running the Castello during my absence, and while Vincent was playing footsie in Milano? Leonora, that's who! The baby of the family showed the most sense of all. Now do you understand why I'm worried?"

"I sure see your point. Ah, I do get it! That's why Leonora was so gracious to Vince after those fights. You're saying that she has a good grasp on the whole picture, right?"

"Exactly! Most important, she never got any instructions from me. She picked up the mantle only because she understood that nobody else would. She had the insight, and the guts to do it."

"Why, then, do you need Vince?"

"To protect HER!"

"So Vince is to be her bodyguard?"

"Oh, come on! Vince is to be the Duke, and he must understand that in the performance of his ducal duties he can rely on the good sense of his cousin Leonora. That's what I want to see happening."

"OK, now we're on the same page. I'll talk to Vince while he's under my roof, and see to it that he has the whole picture as well as I understand it myself. He'll still have to rely on you."

"He'll have more help than he'll ever need. I don't know what I'd do without him. There's a lot of good stuff in him."

"And some bad stuff. He can be as stubborn as a mule!"

"Perfect! I don't want to see him easily led. I'm giving him Carte Blanc to kick ass whenever he has to. I'm turning him loose on them, but I won't put it in exactly those words. He must not lose respect for ME!"

"That he won't do. He's seen enough to know that you're his superior, so he'll be a good boy that way."

"Fine! Oh, and tell him Gilda loves him. I'm pretty sure she does."

He laughed. "You're still in the driver's seat. God help us all."

Piero had that right. I'll move Heaven and Hell to keep the duchy together.

Chapter Ten

Vince's Third Florida Visit

Vince called me a week after his surgery. I asked him how his hand was healing and he said it was coming along fine.

"The doctors fixed whatever it was that was causing me so much pain. I can't wait to have the free use of my hand again."

"So that you'll be ready to punch somebody else?"

"Oh, no, uncle, I've learned my lesson. From now on I'll hire someone else to do the punching, like you did with your two Sicilians."

"Well, now you're getting smart. When are you going back to Italy?"

"Am I going back? Do you still trust me to fill your place?"

"Yes, of course! Come here first. I want to spend some time with you. We'll enjoy some laughs."

"What's so funny?"

"Vince, when I first went to Italy to take over, I was greener that you are now. You have the experience of your Bounty Hunting days to back you. For me it was on-the-job training, and if it wasn't for Count Villano we would have lost our shirts."

"That bad, huh?"

"Was it ever! For most of my years there I was convinced that I was looking failure in the face. I felt that dark cloud over my head every day. I was miserable most of the time. Villano and my sweet Laura helped me hold it together."

"You really loved her, didn't you?"

"Not at first. Love came slowly, but when it took she became my whole world, just as Gilda will become yours"

"I wouldn't count on that, uncle."

"What are you saying?"

"I'm not sure I'm saying anything. I think it will be enough if I just get used to her. What does she have the right to expect?"

"To be loved, idiot! No one can force you to love her, but you'd damned well better be kind to her. You have to be her MAN, make no mistake about that!"

"I fully intend to be her man! She'll know she's got a man when she gets the full treatment. When I take her into the bedroom I'll ask her to take a good look at the floor."

"Why?"

"Because all she'll see is the ceiling for the first week! You never heard that old joke?"

"If I did, I had forgotten it. So that's your game plan huh?"

"Uncle, I've got the horns for it. That you can rely on."

"Oh, I believe it. Come to Florida. We have a lot to talk about."

"Just as soon as I can, uncle."

One of the main things I wanted in life at this point was peace and quiet, but I found myself feeling impatient for the day Vince would arrive. I began to understand the personal power of the young man, and I was beginning to respect it.

When I first arrived in Italy I began barking orders and worrying everyone in the castle. I had a sour attitude because I was angry, and soon some of the people started to fight back in little ways, making me all the more miserable. With Vince it was going to be different. He is quick to get the measure of people and will soon have them eating out of his hand.

When they sense the inner power of the man they will begin to respect him too. He may break a few things, but at least he will lead.

I called Giulio Villano. "Giulio, my nephew Vince is going to work out well, but he takes some getting used to. I wonder if you would mind taking him under your wing without letting him know you're doing it. He will smash a lot less crockery if you guide him in a subtle way. What do you think?"

"I love the idea! I'll befriend him and do a little steering. It will take him a while for him to catch on, but when he does, I'm sure he'll appreciate the humor in it all. Why should he mind if the results are to his liking?"

"I think you've got him pegged. If he finds you to be the friend that I did, then I can die a contented man."

"Are you thinking of dying?"

"No, but I feel so weary on some days. Don't forget, we've been through a lot. I don't know if I could ever live through those days again. At any rate, I deserve a rest."

"Antonino, you've BEEN resting. Maybe you're getting lazy!"

"Could be! I'll take that under advisement. How are the kids doing? Are they still playing politics in Rome?"

"Yes, and they're having a grand time. I'm afraid they're becoming political animals. They're in the thick of everything and become a force to be reckoned with. We may be able to profit from it some day."

I had to laugh. "Leave it up to you to see the profit in everything. Believe me, my friend, I'll never forget how you pulled my chestnuts out of the fire on several occasions."

"Don't mention it. We had fun, didn't we?"

"Yes, while I was trembling in my boots!"

"Come on! It wasn't THAT bad, was it?"

"Not ALL of it, but there were those times, like the road blockade in Austria. That whole thing was hairy!"

"AND profitable!"

"There you go again! You're forever irrepressible."

"I just like the sound that money makes. That jingle is music to my ears."

"Yeah! You'll get along with Vince. When you get to know him better, ask him about the raids. I'm telling you, you're going to respect him, wait and see."

"Don't keep me in suspense. What raids?"

"Oh, I may as well let the cat out of the bag. He and his fellow Bounty Hunters would raid drug operations and take their money. I'll tell you what! When I'm finished writing of his exploits, I'll send you a copy of the book, O.K?"

"I'd love to read it."

"Always nice talking to you Giulio. Let's do this often."

"Let's! Antonino, you should have never retired."

"Perhaps you're right. Talk to you soon, now that we have an interesting project going." I heard Giulio chuckle.

I decided to tell Vince of my conversation with Villano when he gets here. I strongly feel the two of them will become fast friends, and they'll enjoy swapping stories. I'm sure Villano will tell of our exploits over the years, and that should cement their friendship, and Vince will understand a lot more about me and the job I had to do on my watch. It may give him some perspective when doing his own work.

There are some things the secretary, Marco di Dante, will not be able to tell Vince because he came to the job after most of it was over. The former secretary, Ruggiero, would have been able to give Vince chapter and verse concerning all the ins and outs of the bad times. May the dear old man rest in peace!

I can only hope that Rugierro and my lovely wife Laura are having interesting conversations in God's Heaven. I still feel the pain of losing them, even to this day.

When Vince arrived in the cab, I felt elated. There was no doubt in my mind that he was my kind of company. He had a way of listening to you and digesting every word, sometimes divining the meaning even before you've finished you sentence.

He gave me a big smile as he grabbed his luggage and asked, "Well, uncle, are you ready for round three?"

I was more than ready. No sooner had he dumped his bags in his room I gave him the latest news from Italy. "Regina delivered her baby, a son."

"So soon? I thought she had some time yet."

"No, she went the full term. They are naming him Leonello."

"Why that name?"

"After one of the early Ferrarese Dukes who was known for advancing the arts. Talking about art, I think I'll do your portrait while you're here"

"You don't have a studio."

"These glass doors face north. We'll make it do!"

"Leonello! It has a nice ring to it. Too bad the baby was born under a cloud."

"Why do you say that, Vince?"

"Uncle, I don't think things are going to go well with Vincenti. He's got a twist in his head, and he bears watching."

"Let's hope he'll settle down now with his wife and baby. He must understand that this is his last hope for a decent life. Besides, I don't think there's anything he can screw up in Neunkirchen."

"I hope you're right, but I have an uncomfortable feeling about him. He has the restless devil in him."

"Ah, Vince, just leave him alone. He'll be under Terzo's wing."

"Yeah, you're right!" but Vince said that without any conviction. Those two are on a collision course, and we'll be lucky if something doesn't blow up.

For a few days we chatted about inconsequential things while he sat for the portrait, but then Vince asked a strange question. "Uncle, do you think Isabella and Sister Monica will ever want to come out of the convent?"

"Where did THAT question come from? They seem to be doing all right where they are. What do you have in mind?"

"Nothing, really. It's just that it seems to me they would both serve the family better if they lived in the Castello. Why would anyone voluntarily have themselves locked away from their family and friends, and the freedom of normal society?"

"That's a question I've asked myself many times. We think alike, Vince. No, I don't think they'll want to come out. If you ask me, it's a form of cowardice, running away from the world. Maybe it makes them feel secure, I sure don't know."

"What a shame! How pretty Isabella is."

We said no more about it, but I knew it would be something he'd have in his mind for a long time to come. He didn't like the idea of family members being in the convent. We DO think alike! It's amazing.

We talked about his return to Italy, and how he should try to befriend Count Giulio Villano. "If for no other reason you'll like and admire him as a friend, but remember, he can get things done, even some things you may think impossible."

"I'm sure I can use a friend like that."

"Yes you can. Now, tell me, how soon after you return to Italy do you want to get married?"

"Can that wait a while?"

"No! You'll need companionship and loving. I want someone there for you when you get one of your mindless erections."

"Uncle! If you please!" then we both laughed. He knew I wasn't being fooled by his "modesty". Then he shrugged and said, "Maybe I can pin down one of the maids."

"I don't recommend it."

"You're right, of course. How about if I go into Monza and find a girl there?"

"Oh yes, and no one will EVER know! Testa dura! (Hard head!) No joking now. When do you want to get married?"

"How about after I test Gilda out? O.K, no joking! I don't know, but the question more is, when I get married, do I also become the Duke?"

"So, you tie those two issues together?"

"Well yes! My father said that's the way it should be or I might be out flapping in the wind some day."

"And he's right! We have to secure your succession. Let me think on this and I'm sure everything will work out to everyone's satisfaction and protection. I'm putting the final touches on the new contract now. Talk to Gilda as soon as you can."

"Why? She'll have to accept what comes if she wants this marriage."

"Women have to set the date, dummy! When you go to poking around, you don't want to run into a rag."

"I didn't think of that. O.K. I'll have to talk to her anyway. I'll do that when I get back to New York. She'll be calling Francesca anyway, so I'll take the opportunity then."

"Yes, feel her out. No, I didn't mean THAT way!"

Chapter Eleven

A Family Gathering

Once back in New York Vince called and told me the latest ex-rays showed his hand was healing nicely, and that he'll be able to get out of the cast soon. I asked him if he spoke to Gilda, and he said, "No, but Francesca asked her about a marriage date, and Gilda said she didn't know."

"Let it hang there for the moment. At least she'll think about it now."

"OK! I'm thinking about packing for my trip to Italy, but I want to have some time here with my old friends."

"Now you stay out of trouble! I know you. You're itching for action, aren't you?"

"In fact an old boss asked me for some help. There will be no danger for me, I just have been asked to plan a defense of a warehouse, and I'll be heading up the team who will do the work."

"I knew it! The minute you arrive in New York you're humping the girls and running with that den of thieves. Will I ever be able to trust you to toe the mark?"

"I'm towing, Uncle! Don't worry about this one. I'll be in no danger, and I'll make a bundle."

"Damn you, Vince! You keep me on the edge of my chair. You'd better be right on this. I'll do something fierce if you get hurt."

"Uncle, let's change the subject. What shall I do when I get to Italy? Are there any special instructions?

"Just stay out of trouble. Socialize for a while. Don't push anything. Relax. Show them you're not the dragon and nobody will call Saint George to slay you."

"I'm glad Leonora is on my side."

"They ALL are. Just give them a chance. How many times do I have to repeat this? They are Italians! Go with the flow! Get with the program! Mi capisce?"

"Si! Capisco!"

"At last! Now when you go have fun, and drink a little wine. That will refresh your spine."

"My spine?"

"It's an old Italian saying which means that a little wine will improve everything about you. Have a nice trip, and call me when you get there."

"O.K."

"Who are these chat friends?"

"People I met on MY SPACE."

"Any serious attachments?"

"There's one lady that's very interesting, but we'll never meet."

"Good! Remember your social standing."

"No problem, uncle."

Vince reported that he checked out the old warehouse for his old boss and saw it could use some security improvements.

"The boss followed my thinking and allowed me to contact some people who would make the necessary improvements.

"I was able to assemble almost the same crew we used before, and soon we had settled in to wait for the expected raid. The old building was a surprise to me. I didn't know there were any of these dinosaurs around anymore. All the other ones were either torn down or completely renovated.

"There was an old room that was once used as an office, and miraculously the refrigerator, the small stove and the sink still worked. The room was filthy, and the place that passed as a bathroom was even filthier.

"Some of the men brought beer despite my instructions about alcohol while on the job. 'It's just light beer.' One of them said, but surely, after a few beers they'll want a woman, just like they did on the last job we were on.

"I didn't ask how anyone knew there would be an attempt to rob the warehouse. There didn't seem like there was anything worth stealing.

"Well, I just assumed the boss knew what he was talking about and he did.

"On the second night we heard somebody jimmying one of the windows on the ground floor. The boys started to move forward, but I signaled them to step back and be quiet.

"I whispered, to the men, 'I want them to come in.'" The boys moved back into the shadows and waited. These guys breaking in were so clumsy that it took them some time to get the heavy wire frame open and they made enough noise doing it to wake up the dead.

"They noisily slipped in and got ready to look around. When they opened their flashlights they saw us, and the guns pointed at them. One of them said, 'Oh man! ---Oh, shit!'

"I showed my crew how I wanted them trussed up, and they soon had the burglars tied up in neat cocoons. Let me describe my cocoons. The bad guy is first bound at the wrists behind his back with either a rope or handcuffs, then a noose is slipped around his neck, and the long end is passed down his back under the bound wrists, and tied around his ankles after his knees are bent. If he struggles, he tightens the noose and cuts off his own air supply.

"One of the burglars asked if the cops were called, and I said, 'No, we're not going to call them in.'

"'Then what are you going to do?'

"'You're heading for the East river, Bunkie. We're not going to give you the chance to ever come back here.'

"'We won't, I swear to God, we'll never come back.'

"'I KNOW you won't! You'll be too busy swimming.'

"'Please, give us a break! We'll do anything.'

"One of my men pulled me aside and asked, 'What ARE we going to do with them?'

"'We'll just hold them for the boss. Let him make the decisions.'

"'Good! I thought you were going to kill them!'

"'Commit murder just for breaking into an old building? What's the matter with you?'

"Well, you sounded serious."

"The boss did call the police and had the gang hauled away. I grabbed my money and ran. So you see, Uncle? You were concerned about nothing."

"I see, and I also see that that's your last caper. Vince, if I ever have a heart attack, you'll be blamed as being the cause of it, that's for sure!" I heard him laugh and knew he was just playing.

After he arrived at the Castello, Vince called me and said that in the limo traveling to the Castello, he began to think that it might be a good idea to have a conference with the family. Upon arriving there he did call every one of the relatives to the small dining room and was shocked to see that the family still living in the Castello was comprised only of women. It was clear that this family conference wasn't going to amount to much.

"Uncle, There I sat with Leonora, Carlotta, Elena and the aging Countess Colonna. None of the men were available and that was all right with me. Carlotta's husband always seems to avoid family meetings."

"Vincenti is presently right across the Autostrada. Why didn't you call him in?"

"You must be joking! What I wanted to tell the rest of the family has as much to do with him as anything else."

"So what did you want to tell the family?"

"I wanted them to understand that I was not totally convinced that I was the one to follow you in the succession. It continues to prey on my mind that there must be another way, and that perhaps the family could help me out of my dilemma."

"Why do you still harbor doubts? Haven't I made it clear to you that there was no other way? Don't you think I did everything possible to groom Vincenti for the position? Also, you saw how Terzo is. He won't do!"

"Yes, Uncle. That's the conclusion everyone in the Castello came to as well. We went over everything. Leonora, of course, was positive, and Carlotta took no position, but at least she was not opposed. Elena is also in my camp, and the Contessa said she thought everything would work out well."

Leonora spoke for Beatrice who was at the University and conveyed her opposition to my succeeding her father.

"Don't worry about Beatrice! Her bark is worse than her bite. As for the Countess, It looks like she really has mellowed. Maybe the loss of her husband, the Count Colonna has plucked her feathers."

"She was tough on you?"

"She was the bane of my existence. I came close to throwing her out of the Castello on several occasions, but she was, after all, my dear Laura's mother."

"I can say she's OK now.

"Good! So you see the road is clear for you to pick up the mantle and wear it with pride. The very fact that the men are not there is proof enough that your strength is needed there."

"I sure does look that way now."

"So put aside any doubts you may have and roll up your sleeves. Remember what I told you. Everything is quite simple. Most of our income comes from what grows on the land. These products already have buyers, so just see to the crops.

"The pumice mine is a very small operation and is being run by a very capable man who's been doing it for years. The rest is maintenance, and the care of the workers. There is nothing to figure out, and certainly nothing to confound you. Just sit in with Marco di Dante for regular meetings, and that's about it.

"Finally, act like you're taking care of the family. You'll be called on only if there's a dispute, and all you have to do is say a few words and they'll obey. It's really a piece of cake, until something happens to jeopardize the family. All they need is your presence."

"All right. I'm on the job, uncle. You can depend on me."

"Good boy!"

"What abut the Bergamo gang?"

"Put that out of your mind." That's what I told him, but I knew he wouldn't.

When we hung up the phones, I began to wonder if being the Duke would be enough of a challenge for Vince. He was always a man of action, and this might prove to be a giant bore. Then again, he's Thirty now. He should be happy enough to settle down and enjoy some peace of mind. I hope!

Then a letter came from him.

Dear Uncle,

Leonora suggested I get a gift for Leonello, so she bought some clothes for him and we went to visit the proud parents at the Fusco Manor. They showed me the baby with much pride, and I got the impression that both Vincenti and Regina were finally going to grow up into the family structure.

Regina told me that they talked things over, and they are sure they will like their new situation in Neunkirchen. "It will be a fine place for Leonello to grow up and be schooled." She seemed content.

Vincenti said he was looking forward to working with Terzo, so maybe the tension is finally over. I'll reserve any opinion until I see more proof of it.

I spoke to the foreman on the Fusco property and he assures me that everything will be looked after there. He said he was an old hand and could do everything with his eyes closed. He's funny!

So far so good! If there is anything you want me to look into, let me know.

Your nephew, Vince

So it was that many months went by with no cause for concern. The Castello settled down to a simple routine. Vince had to learn what the word "maintenance" meant.

He was kept busy seeing to what the repairmen and the staff was doing as a matter of every day routine, and he told me that when it came time to clean the huge chandeliers in the crystal room he was astounded to see what was involved.

"They were lowered by winches built above the ceiling, and the girls could clean only one chandelier each day when it was time for the cleaning... When the chandeliers were down close to the floor, I realized only then how huge they were. What a job!"

The crystal room goes up almost two stories, and there is a low attic above the ceiling that allows workmen to go to the winches and the dome that tops the foyer. Aside from that crawl space, there is no connection between the north and the south wings on the third floor.

Later, with more mock complaining, he told of how the repairmen were always busy on something. "Fixing, scraping, painting, plastering! My god! It never ends! And that's just the Castello!"

When I spoke to his father, we enjoyed another laugh at Vince's expense. "He's learning!"

Piero wanted to know about the marriage. "We've got to get on that soon. Just let some time go by until we're sure he's going to stick. Right now I'm hoping he doesn't bolt."

"Yes, He's got ants in his pants all right. The newness of his position is keeping him interested for a time, but when the novelty wears off, he'd better have a wife to pin him down."

I had to agree with my brother. Vince was always an adventurer and enjoyed the spirit of the chase. If he gets bored at the Castello, I'll send him to check up on things in Uruguay. He'll like that, and he'll also like Count Cesare. It's time they met again anyway, this time on Vince's own authority. As it was, his social life began to improve. Tinti, my ward, and now Princess Nicolo Pallavicini, invited Vince and Gilda Colonna to dinner at their palace outside of Rome.

Vince was not fooled by it but it afforded him the opportunity to see Gilda. They were seated together at the large table and Vince liked what he saw. She smiled prettily and spoke quietly, and acted almost mousy. She was just nervous.

My Dear Uncle,

    When the invitation came in for me to go to the Pallavicini Palace, I had to scurry around to get a tuxedo. I have never owned one, always thinking that they were strange suits for men to be wearing, but the invitation said "Formal Attire", so I could not argue with that.
    I am flattered, of course, to be invited to such an affair, but as Leonora was helping me chose and wear the tuxedo, she had a smirk on her face that looked like the cat that had eaten the canary.
    I smell a rat! Is this whole thing a put-up job? Come on, uncle, what are the people playing at? With my sincerest apologies, it crossed my mind that your hand is somehow showing here.
    I did meet Tinti during the time you were in the hospital at Monza, but she didn't show me any particular interest. So why now, I wonder!
    Confess, uncle. I say with tongue in cheek that there isn't much that goes on in this world without you approval. Well, at least that's what my father hinted at when I spent those days with my parents.

I'll promise I'll be on my best behavior, but I will be out of my element, that's for certain. Gilda has also been invited, which makes me all the more suspicious that your hand is in this.

I have no idea how big this dinner party is, so maybe if there are a lot of people there I can hide in the shadows and avoid any mistakes. You will be the first to know what transpires at this affair.

Your suspicious nephew. Vince

Poor Vince! His first real test in the social world of the Aristocracy, and he's befuddled. Well, he's on his own. He has to learn, even if it's the hard way. If he has the sense God gave him to use he'll ask Leonora for some pointers. Maybe she'll volunteer to give him some hints. At any rate we'll all have some chuckles over his attempts to make the right impression with the other invitees.

I'll call and give Tinti the "heads-up" so that she can help him survive this ordeal, then report back to me. This should be a howler!

I'm not trying to give Vince a hard time, or to show him up as a rube. I'm just plotting to throw him and Gilda together. There has to be a marriage soon.

My ward wrote:

Your Grace,

I'm most happy to report to you that Vince handled himself with cool aplomb during the whole evening. He was quite gracious and made a nice bow when the Price introduced him to all the others.

He held Gilda's hand and chatted amiably with her, and I think I saw her eyes sparkling. She's falling in love with her "barbarian" after all. If he is rough around the edges, she will polish him in no time.

I'll admit that she's getting a handsome man, and I'll be happy to help Gilda polish his edges!

The only time Vince was distracted was when Deli came out to do her dances. His eyes were riveted on her, and I can almost guess what he was thinking.

With careful observation one can detect a raw power about him. He moves like a cat. As he studied the scene, there wasn't much that escaped his notice. He was especially interested in Count Villano. I could see his eyes following the Count around the room at times. When they met, he pumped the Count's hand firmly.

Vince may not be used to these parties, but he's certainly not afraid of anything. People looked at his hand but said nothing about it. Why would they? Everyone knew the story anyway.

He carried the night! All were interested in this new Duke, and no doubt wondering what he has up his sleeve for the future. You need not worry about him, my Lord. He'll do real well. Do you think he suspects anything?

Your loving Tinti

    Indeed he does! Vince is trained to be suspicious of everything, and has eyes like a hawk. His notes on his work suggested to me that he could see in the dark. It wouldn't surprise me if he could see through walls, if you know what I mean.
    I learned later that he also made inquiries about Giovanni Fusco, discreetly of course, so as not to upset Tinti. I'll have to ask Vince why he was interested in Giovanni, but I can almost guess.
    Giovanni was a jailbird, and Vince was only keeping his eyes peeled. He keeps his radar working at all times. Giovanni was not at the dinner, lucky for him. Vince would have burned holes in him with his eyes.

    Vince wrote me, anxious to let me know that he fit in with the snooty crowd at the dinner: I already had Tinti's letter, so it was interesting to see what Vince had to say about it.

Dear Uncle,

    I didn't make a fool of myself at the dinner and thought I carried it off well enough. People were interested in me and asked some simple questions. I could see they were tying to be nice and I answered their questions in the simplest way possible. My Italian is not that good, but they were forgiving and understanding. It's true that Italians are happy when you try to speak the language.

It was Count Villano who asked me a question that threw me off balance. He wanted to know if I intended to join the Monarchists and I responded that I didn't know enough about them. We didn't chat too long. He had to get to everybody. Quite a social lion, isn't he?

What should I know, uncle? Are the Monarchists scheming against anything? I don't relish being caught in the middle of anything I don't understand, or of which I cannot approve.

Gilda looked so nice in her black ballroom gown, a little low cut, and she wore a simple string of pearls, but she looks so young! Is she ready for marriage? She doesn't look it. As I looked at her I kept thinking that this girl was to be my wife, and I shall have to teach her how to be a woman. Or does that come naturally to females?

The dancer Deli sure knows how to throw her treasures around. Even with the lovely Gilda at my side, I couldn't help the feeing that I would like to poke Deli with the joystick one day. She may be older but she's the most grateful.

About the dinner generally, I must say that the food was excellent, as I expected it would be, but I can't help feeling that the whole evening was overdone. There was just too much of everything. These affairs can be managed in a much more simple way. It was overkill!

It's clear that these gatherings are made so that the women can show off their finery. What other purpose do they serve? Well, perhaps the men get together and make their deals. I don't know.

Did you have to put up with these affairs often? Did you have to give big parties at the Castello? I hope I don't have to get involved in all that. I'd hate it! I won't allow this job to turn me into a fop!

What is your advice?

Your nephew, Vince

Oh, stop it Vince, I thought to myself! You don't have to analyze everything to death. Go with the flow! Just do your thing. Don't you get it yet? I didn't tell HIM that, though. In fact, I didn't tell him anything. He has to get used to the way things are done and to stop worrying about it. He just feels that he's on shaky ground when he actually isn't.

Later on I received a letter that indicated that he was settling in much better. These things take time, and now he's beginning to realize that. His letter said:

Dear Uncle,

The apartment at the Villa Laura is ready to receive Vincenti and Regina and little Leonello. In fact they are moving as I write. I will be going with them to Neunkirchen to oversee the move, and to dampen any arguments Vincenti may want to make. If he causes any trouble, I'll be there to step on him.

I want to see a respite from the workmen's noises in the Castello. When they have finished refurbishing the rooms they are working on now, I want to send them packing for a while. They are making a career of fussing around the Castello and bellying up to the trough. This is not a civil service job!

Uncle, how did you spend your off time around here? I cannot help notice that my personal maid has a really cute ass. How about it, uncle! Just one for the Gipper! Just kidding you know!

Vince

I called him. "Vince, there are a lot of things you can do to occupy your time. Take a drive around the land and see what the field workers are doing. At this time of year there are a lot of preparations being made for the growing season. Show yourself to the workers, and learn something about the crops.

"You'll soon see how interesting it is to follow the growing and the picking seasons. Some day you can go to Como and see how they prepare the tables for the silk worms, and how the silk is produced.

"You'll also be amazed when the wheat is harvested. You'll see sights you've never seen before. On the Bergamo property you'll see how the wheat is milled and bagged. Villano has his trucks take the flour bags to market, so you don't have to worry about that. Just bank the checks he sends you.

"You can LOOK at the maid's cute ass, but that's all. If you need your nookie, get married!"

Vince called me and said that Gilda had come for lunch, and when he got her alone in the Crystal Room they sat in a love seat and he started kissing her. She was quiet responsive, but some workers came through the room and spoiled the mood.

I'm really going to send them packing any day now.

Chapter Twelve

Vince Grows Horns

Vince called and told me that the new apartment for Vincenti and his family at the Villa Laura was plain, but very roomy. "They should be happy here. They will want for nothing. I recommended to both Terzo and Vincenti that they look around and find what work Vincenti will enjoy doing. He has a regular smorgasbord to choose from. He should find something to his liking.

"My soft warning was a reminder that idleness is the devil's plaything. How am I doing?"

"You're doing well, Vince. I think you can leave that situation to Terzo now. You'll have other fish to fry. How about taking Gilda to a show?"

"Not a bad idea, if her school schedule will allow for that right now."

"She can make the time. Don't take "No" for an answer. You're supposed to be wooing her. Get cracking!"

"Uncle, you're a real matchmaker at heart."

"And YOU are a horny toad! We must get you both to the altar. Tinti writes that Gilda has fallen in love with you and the girl may be getting the itch herself. Set your mind to this. You must begin to see the urgency of it for the sake of the family, and the local populace."

"Quite honestly, uncle, I don't understand this urgency. First of all Gilda wants to finish school. She's made that clear. She wants to start her career as a psychologist and I do believe she has her heart set on that.

"Then uncle, there's another thing you may not be aware of. She mentioned at the dinner that she doesn't want to be separated from her parents. We have to factor that in to this equation. She very young and not given to any adventures."

"Vince, start thinking of taking control! You're being rather namby-pamby about Gilda and not thinking ahead. Sure she wants a career. That's no surprise! She's in school and entranced by her books and studies.

"Motherhood will knock all those fancy ideas out of her head. Right now she wants to change the world, but the moment she realized she's with child, she'll want nothing else but her baby.

"What have you learned about women while playing with your big-city playmates? Did none of them ever give you even the faintest hint that they wanted babies? Tell me the truth! Or didn't you ever notice that?"

"Yes, uncle, they did talk about babies, but I never took that seriously. What my playmates, as you call them, wanted was no concern of mine as long as we got our rocks off in good style. I'm not so ready for fatherhood. What's the big deal there?"

"The future! If we were not talking about the future and working for that, then you may as well go back to New York and become a tennis bum. The family must continue, as every family must, not only our own. But we have special responsibilities. We hold our history in our hands and the history of the nation as well."

"The nation? How so?"

"What do you suppose made Italy what it is? It's the Aristocracy and all that it has represented in the past, and holds for the future. It was the Aristocracy that gave Italy its special flavor. No other nation on earth is like Italy. Everyone discovers that sooner or later."

"I think it's going to take time for me to fully understand what you're saying. Italy is nice, but I'm not sure what you mean by "special flavor" and the difference between Italy and other countries. Doesn't every country have its own "special flavor"?"

"No! It's true every country is different, but no country matches Italy for its culture and its people. No nation has such richness in its very soul."

"I'll need time to come to your conclusions. Should I look for it, and how will I know it when I see it?"

"Don't look for it. It will seep into your own soul soon enough. After a while, when you return to the United States, you'll immediately miss the soul of Italy. That's when you'll understand what I mean. The United States is the greatest country in the world, but it doesn't have a soul."

"Uncle, them's fightin' words in some parts!"

"Enough! Go and see Gilda! If you spend enough time with her we'll soon be cutting the wedding cake."

"It may comfort you to know that I WANT to see her. I don't love her, but she gives me the "hots". Talk to you soon, uncle."

Every woman gives him the "hots"! If Gilda does not want to leave her parents, we can have THEM move into the Castello degli Estensi. Why not? There's enough room there now, what with my kids scattered to the four winds.

I fervently hope that Vincenti will settle down now. I guess we'll never know what it is about him that keeps him in hot water all the time. Is he just a bad seed? Is that what I have to conclude? Maybe he has a touch of insanity in addition to being stupid.

Well, a father can plant the seed, and his mother can give him birth, but after that it's a crapshoot. No matter what one does, and no matter what privileges the child enjoys, he'll grow in his own way, and there's not much anyone can do about it.

Should a father continue to hope? Isn't there a point where a father just gives up and closes his eyes to the child's fate? I think I've gotten to that point. If Vincenti muddies the water in Neunkirchen, then I quit! Enough is enough!

Besides, if Vince and Gilda give us some nice strong boys the whole issue will be moot. Yes, a few healthy boys will secure the future for the House of Este. I'm already seeing it in my mind. Three, maybe four big boys to carry the ball for te family well into the future. Well, I can dream, can't I?

Another letter from Vince:

Dear Uncle,

Following your advice to date Gilda, I decided I'd visit her at the University and see her in the school environment. I didn't hit any students there this time.

When I went the office and told them who I was and the purpose of my visit, a student was assigned to take me directly to her class. When I walked in, the students, seeing me immediately knew who I was, and a hushed "Oh!" went through the class. The professor told Gilda she was excused, but I told him I'd sit and wait for the class to end.

The professor went on with the lesson, and I listened to a lot of psychobabble while poor Gilda blushed red.

When the class was over, I found myself surrounded by wide-eyed girls asking a bunch of questions that I never got a chance to answer. The boys stood aside looking on and wondering what to make of it all.

I guess I was some kind of hero, or perhaps a barbarian to be feared. It took a while to get Gilda by the hand and lead her off.

She suggested we go to the student's cafeteria, but the student's professor recommended the teachers lunchroom. He led us there and sat with us while we had a bite, I suppose to legitimize our presence there.

Afterward we walked around the campus chatting and some of the girls whistled. What's this world coming to?

She agreed that we might start actual dating and would take up the subject with her father. I behaved myself all the while, but had the strongest urge to reach over and play with her cute tits.

Uncle, being a gentleman is much harder than I thought. Tell me, do you really expect me to be celibate during this protracted period? Shall I look for a monastery to hide in?

Talk to me, please! Vince

OH boy! This Vince has HORNS! This is going to be a sticky wicket, but every problem has a solution, I believe, so I'll work on this and find a way.

Reviewing things in my mind, I made a decision. I would send him Deli. I notified Tinti to tell Deli to go to the Castello and make my studio her bedroom. Deli understood, and was hot to trot. When she lived in the Castello she was getting reamed regularly, and as far as I know she didn't have much going on sexually at the Pallavicino Palace.

When Deli was informed, she did a happy dance around her room and was packed in a trice. When she was nicely ensconced in the studio, and Vince saw her dance for the household, nature took it's course and in the middle of the night, Vince was on her and in her. She cooperated in every way.

(Nine months later she gave birth to a boy, Armal! Who knew she was fertile? The moment it was discovered that Deli was pregnant, and as soon as everyone got over their surprise, Prince Nocolo wanted to arrange a quick marriage between Deli and Giovanni Fusco, the "jailbird." No one liked the idea, especially Princess Tinti, so the Prince sensibly scrapped any thought of that.

Vince never mentioned it to me, and I don't know if he suspected my hand in this, but it must have occurred to him that the opportunity to join with Deli in the studio was a little more than serendipitous.

Leonora reported that when the two lovebirds didn't come down for breakfast it indicated that the fire was still burning.

The maid reported that when she took a breakfast tray to Vince's bedroom, she found them bathing in the tub together.

Beatrice wrote:

Dear Father,

Have you taken leave of your senses? Do you mean to turn the Castello into a whorehouse? If Vince must behave like a satirist and Deli a Messalina, could they not go to New York and do their rutting there?

How are we expected to keep this a secret from Gilda and her family? Honestly father, in your zeal to secure the future of the family, you're making a laughing stock of all of us.

The man is a monster! There's no other way to describe him. Instead of being our savior, he will undo us all. I'm flabbergasted at your latest maneuver. Really father, do something to preserve our dignity.

Your loving daughter, Beatrice

I might have known that Beatrice would be the one to complain. She's the brightest of my children, but also prudish, and a general pain-in-the-ass! What she knows about men can be written on the head of a pin.

I wrote to Beatrice, saying that, if she prefer, I can have Vince marry Deli, and SHE will be the new Duchess of the Castello. I asked her if she thought that was a better plan, and in the absence of any real ideas on her part, I recommended that she mind her own business and leave the policy of the family to me where it rightfully belongs. Be happy that Vince doesn't try to bed YOU down, I warned her.

Beatrice will discuss this letter with the family and they will talk it to death, but no one will come up with any solutions. Well, I didn't think so, anyway.

Leonora wrote:

Dear father,

I am not going to listen to Beatrice's protestations about Vince's behavior. I told her quite emphatically that Vince is not married and further, is accustomed to regular lovemaking. She must understand that an active man cannot be turned off like a faucet.

She's incensed that you would say that Vince might desire HER at some point. Honestly father, I never could see what's in your mind. Do you think Vince would ever carnally desire ME?

Father, it might be a good idea to start thinking about a husband for me. Please don't be shocked, and don't preach, but I find myself being jealous of Deli and what she is getting in the studio.

I do feel a sense of shame, and I will pray to find the strength to clear my mind, but there's no doubt that Vince is a handsome man. We have always been honest with each other, so you must not think badly of me for confessing what is part of my nature.

Have no fear that I will dishonor the family. Still it's close to the time when I should marry.

Your loving daughter, Leonora

It never ends! My own baby in heat! There will come a day, and it better be soon, that these problems will be for Vince to solve. If I think I'm retired, then I'm living in a fool's paradise. I wrote to Leonora:

Dearest Daughter,

Has it been that many years since my baby daughter was a little girl? It comes as a surprise to me that you, of all my children should be speaking of marriage. I must face the truth. You're all grown up and with a good head on your shoulders. If you are having womanly feelings, then who am I to say differently?

Be assured that I will not preach. Indeed, I must confess something to you myself. I would have been disappointed if you did NOT have womanly feelings toward Vince. He seems to exude that manly magnetism most men wish they had.

I know you will not dishonor the family, but my sweet child, whom shall you marry? Can you wait a while? You ARE still quite young, despite your hormonal urgings. Marriage is serious business, so grit your teeth and wait until were all better prepared for your nuptials.

Besides, we really should see Beatrice married first, don't you think? After all, she's the third born, and you're the sixth!

What is your opinion of her man Francesco? Is he the wimp he seems to be? He has an Aristocratic background, but he may have become one of those air-headed liberals we see in so many colleges these days.

Your Loving Father

Chapter Thirteen

A Fatal Mistake

Of course it didn't take long for me to get more bad news from Neunkirchen. Terzo reported that Regina is crying her eyes out and wants Vincenti to spend more time at home with her and the baby.

It seems as though Vincenti chose to work with the lumbermen in the forest, and was spending too many nights in the cabin there. When Terzo went to tell Vincenti to go to his wife, he found him and a young lumberman playing footsie with an under-age girl from a Contadina family. She was sitting on the workman's lap with her legs canted up, and Vincenti was pumping his hose well up into her furrow.

Terzo, with smoke coming out of his ears, put the two men and the girl in the truck and drove to a point near the girl's house. She had sneaked out through a window to meet the men, so Terzo told her to sneak back in the same way and to keep her mouth shut.

He then drove back to the Villa Laura and locked the two men in a chicken coop. Then he called me.

"Father, Regina wants to go back to her parent's house. All hell is going to break loose! I don't know what my next move should be."

"Take Regina back to the Castello degli Estensi! Say nothing to her parents, and prevent her from doing so too. Tell Vince what happened and abide by his decisions. Keep me posted.

"All right, father. I'm on the way."

I next heard from Vince. "Uncle, I sent Deli back to the Pallavicini Palace and then rushed to the Villa Laura. The secretary Marco di Dante is notifying Count Cesare in Uruguay that I'm on the way with two workers for him, and is also making flight arrangements." If I get a direct flight, I should be there in no time."

I told him, "When you arrive, stay put! I'll meet you there! It is my job to deal with Vincenti!"

The flight to Montevideo was uneventful, but I was so distracted by the latest events that I barely noticed anything, and refused to eat the meal the flight attendant placed before me.

When we arrived at the airport there was transportation waiting for me and we sped to the Hacienda d'Este in the Maldonado area near the Punta del Este.

There was no disguising my rage at Vincenti. This was the last straw! I asked for a horsewhip, and had Vince walk Vincenti and me deep into the Pecan Grove. There I had Vince tie Vincenti's wrists together over a tree branch, and told Vince to go back to the Hacienda.

Vincenti was whining and pleading for Vince to intercede on his behalf, but Vince had his own ax to grind and ignored Vincenti's protestations.

When I was sure Vince was out of earshot, I laid into Vincenti with the whip. He howled piteously, and I guess he fainted at about the fifteenth lash, but I laid on five more for myself. Even as he hung there unconscious I said. "You are disowned, and out of the family. No one shall speak your name again."

Back at the Hacienda, I apologized to Count Cesare d'Este for the lack of courtesy on my arrival,

He said, "I understand! I saw the blood in your eyes and knew you had to do what you had to do. Welcome to the Hacienda, Your grace. It's been too long."

"You'd better send someone to bring him back here before some animals eat him."

"Very well!"

When Vincenti was brought back he was put into the workmen's barracks and left to suffer without treatment. I told Cesare that he should never mention his name. "Call him 'Malandrino'. That should be good enough for him."

We stayed as long as we could at the Hacienda, but I wanted to go home, and Vince had to get back to the Castello.

Unfortunately that wasn't the end of it. Count Cesare called me one day and said that the 'Malandrino' had escaped, and wanted to know if he should institute a search.

I said, "No, close the book on him. He was the son I never should have had. I cry, but not for losing him. I cry for the memory of his sainted mother. If she is looking down at my actions, then God help me!"

"Later Vince said that he had the expertise and could track him down even through the jungle, but I insisted that we just let the whole matter go and forget the 'Malandrino' ever existed. "We are well rid of him" I said.

"What about Regina and Leonello?"

"We'll have them live in the Castello and raise Leonello there. After all, they ARE d'Este's and they belong to us."

"Yes, uncle, I believe that's the best course. Leonora and Regina are getting along just fine, and Beatrice will see to her too. Everybody loves little Leonello. I mean everybody! Gilda has been visiting, and is doting on the baby. I think she's baby minded."

"Of course she is. She changed her plans once she started thinking of motherhood?"

"I think women are nuts that way."

"Don't argue with nature. Most females start thinking about their own babies even when they are babies themselves. Yes, even before they realize where babies come from. It's an instinct."

"Do men have a similar instinct?"

"No. A man's instincts come into play when he must protect his own world."

"I guess the 'Malandrino' didn't have that instinct."

"No he didn't. He was totally selfish."

"I wonder what happened to him."

"That's not our concern. Let's not talk of him anymore."

"All right, uncle.! As I used to say in my reports, 'Case closed!'"

A letter came from Vince. He wants to get MARRIED!

Dear Uncle,

The relationship between Gilda and me is heating up, but not through any actions of mine. Gilda is glassy-eyed and keep touching my arms and face. She is always proffering her lips to be kissed, and I keep reminding her that she must be modest at all times.

The problem is with me. If I do hold and kiss her, my erection goes into an automatic pumping motion. If we don't marry soon, I'll probably take her cherry in a moment of frenzy.

Can we have a simple wedding in the chapel? I'm sure Father Alessi will perform the ceremony in minutes, and I can deflower this panting girl behind the altar. Please hurry your response.
Vince

Dear Nephew,

Send Gilda packing! The contract is not ready yet, so you'd better send for Deli again or take cold showers. I wouldn't be opposed if you could put it to Regina, except that she's your cousin by marriage and a close friend of Beatrice's, so she's off limits. That's a shame, because she's been married and would probably love a touch of the brush!

I know you're in a bind, you satirist, but there's nothing for it. You have to get control of yourself. One thing you don't need as the new Duke is the reputation that your brains are in your pants.

Your Uncle, Antonino

Vince had better watch it! I don't want THAT bomb going off in the Castello. That's all I need at this critical time. I made some phone calls to the lawyers telling them to make haste on the contract, and I called my brother Piero giving him the latest news.

He said, "I can't understand where Vince got his horns. No one else in the family is such a sex hound. At least not that I KNOW of, Antonino!"

I laughed. "Is that a hint?"

"Nah! Whom would I possibly be referring to?"

"It's true that I did cut a wide swath when I was single. Those were the days! I could have my pick of any of them, and some were real beauties. Sfortunato! Those happy days are over."

"And it's just as well, too. You were lucky not to have gotten jammed up."

"I guess so! Well I still have the memories."

Yes. And the tell-all book you wrote about it."

"Oh, you mean "An American Sheik"? I didn't put half the stuff in that book. We'll leave the rest to the reader's imagination."\

"Is it still on the market?"

"Oh yes! And still selling."

He laughed, "Maybe I should buy a copy."

Chapter Fourteen

Is the Wedding Off?

The marriage contract was completed and a copy sent to Gilda's father for his approval. He conferred with his lawyer and there being no objections, it was approved. Now the wedding plans can go ahead.

The Contessa Colonna begged off, claiming she was too old to get into wedding planning, and anyway Gilda was not HER daughter. Apparently the Contessa didn't realize that Vince's marriage to another Colonna guaranteed that Vince would continue to take care of the Colonna family.

The contract may have required it, and Vince made a promise to do so, but if Gilda had been from another House, there's no telling what Vince might have done in future years. Without a marriage to another Colonna, Vince would have had no reason to feel any loyalty to that family, and he could well have cut them off.

Gilda's parents came to stay at the Castello to help out and Leonora became the prime planner for the rituals. She was acting the part of the Duchess of the Castello, yet would never attain that position unless she found a Duke to marry. There weren't many marriageable Dukes left in Europe.

Gilda was given the choice of a simple wedding in the chapel or a more elaborate one at the Cathedral at Monza where Laura and I were married. She chose the Cathedral, and who can blame her?

When I spoke to Leonora, I wanted her to understand that I wanted a simpler wedding than I had. "I always thought my wedding to your mother was very much overdone. Remember that Vince is not used to a lot of pomp and will only be annoyed by it.

"Keep it modest, yet make it look like a bigger show than it actually is. The church decorations need not be too elaborate. Souvenir seekers will take most of the decorations anyway, so why overspend on them?

"You don't have to invite a lot of people. Keep it close to the family and try to play down the fact that it's a royal wedding. Neither Vince nor Gilda can be said to have a lot of royal friends, so there's no need for capes and family crests.

"Whatever you do, don't advertise. That was one of our big mistakes, and there was a crush of people, causing a real security problem. Let me know how you plan it."

Leonora was curious. "Tell me Father, why are you giving me all these instruction over the phone? Aren't you planning to be here?"

"Why, yes, of course! It's just that I won't get there until just before the wedding date."

"Why not get here much earlier? We miss you so much, father. We need you here, even if it's just for your presence."

"All right, I'll come earlier, but the newlyweds will need my bedroom, so I'll have to sleep somewhere else. Any ideas as to what room I can use?"

"Father, you must have you own room. The newlyweds don't have to stay the night. They must be off on their own honeymoon, and that's something they can plan themselves. I'll ask Vince and Gilda about that."

"Good idea! No doubt they will agree with everything I've suggested. Let me know what they say."

"All right, I'll get back to you soon."

While all this was going on, Vince and Gilda were in a huddle and making their own plans. I was right about Vince not wanting anything fancy, but Gilda and her parents wanted something grand. This was their only child and they desired something memorable.

This started a little tug of war between Vince and the Colonna family. The old Countess Colonna said, "History is repeating itself! There was a similar difference of opinion when your father and mother were getting married" she told Leonora.

'What did you do?"

"We told the men to butt out and leave such things to the women. What do men know about it, anyway?"

"Well, I like your thinking, but my father is the Duke. We can't ignore His wishes."

"Why not? We did that the last time and he shut up about it. We went ahead and did exactly as we pleased."

"You're right, Grandmamma! I'll call father and tell him to leave everything to us." What do men know about such things?" and they laughed for some ten minutes."

I know about this because my baby Leonora reported every word verbatim. "Father, why should you worry about anything? Leave it to the people in the Castello. That's the best way."

"All right. Then I'll come a few days before the wedding. That's what I wanted to do in the first place. Just be careful. Don't rile Vince because he knows what he likes and will have things pretty much his way. Don't get too fancy-shmancy! He's a force to be reckoned with. Warn the Witch of Endor not to press him."

She chuckled. "You shouldn't call her the Witch of Endor anymore. She's really very sweet."

"That's good news!"

"You're very sweet too, papa. I love you."

"I love you too, my precious baby!"

Leonora reported that at dinner one night everyone was talking about the wedding, but Vince sat quietly listing to all the noise. Finally, the people there realized that Vince was not contributing to the conversation and they suddenly stopped and looked over at him.

His face was steely, and all he said was, "The wedding is off!" Everyone was stunned, to say the least. Too late did they realize that my warning was serious, and that Vince was about to kick the whole thing over.

It was Gilda who asked, "What's the matter?"

"I'll tell you what the matter is. Nobody runs my life! Do you all think I'm some puppet with strings attached? The wedding is OFF!"

"But don't you want to marry me?" Gilda asked, her face showing shock.

"Of course, but does our getting married have to turn into some kind of circus? Are you all mad?"

"But Vince, weddings take some planning. We have to have some ritual and some ceremony. All weddings have those."

"Why?"

"Well, so that everyone will remember the occasion."

"Why should we care who remembers it?"

"But Vince, everything has to be pretty!" she was losing the argument and she knew it, and burst our crying.

Her mother went to her and embraced her, saying, "Don't fret, Baby! You're going to have a nice wedding, and we'll take many pictures. Vince will like that, don't worry."

Leonora sidled over to Vince and said, sotto voce, "If you don't stop being a boor, I'm going to punch you in the nose!"

That broke the ice. Vince nearly fell off his chair laughing. Finally he said, between busts of laughter, "All right we'll have a pretty wedding."

Poor Gilda. She was staring with her mouth agape at this strange man who was soon to be her husband. "Mother, I will never understand him!"

"You will, my angel. Men are not hard to understand once you understand that they are simple minded."

Chapter Fifteen

Vincenti Kaput!

Vince wrote:

Dear Uncle,

I must ask you about a serious matter, and I swear to you that the issue shall remain between us. It involves what transpired at the Hacienda in Uruguay.

During our stay there I noticed you were chatting for quite a while with a man I didn't recognize, but who seemed to be on rather familiar terms with you.

I thought very little of it at the time, assuming that he was one of the men who had something to do with the administration of the business at the property in the Punta del Este.

While looking through some photographs here at the Castello I saw this same man among the group sitting in the office here, and asked who the man was.

I learned that he was one of your invaluable Sicilian Guards, Manolo, who assisted you in many of your adventures during your tenure here in Italy.

At first it didn't make sense until I found out that Manolo fell in love with a girl living at the Hacienda in Uruguay, and that you gave him permission to marry her.

Again, I thought nothing of it, until the news came that Vincenti had escaped from the Hacienda compound.

Dear Uncle, I apologize for the way my mind works, but from what I saw at the compound it is not an easy place to escape from.

I added two plus two and it comes out five! I'm sorry, but I do not see Vincenti escaping on his own, or if he escaped at all. You must forgive me, but I did some digging and came up with a different scenario.

I learned that your Guard Manolo had a way of making people "faint". Taking all this, and adding the fact that you didn't want anyone go out to search for Vincenti makes me arrive at only one conclusion. Don't get me wrong. If he's gone I'll sleep better. I don't want him at my back.

Shall I spell it out Uncle? Most respectfully, Vince

I wasn't surprised that Vince figured it out. His training automatically comes into play whenever he smells a rat, and he smelled a rat in this case. He is too smart by halves, but that does not anger me. It only re-affirms my choice in him as the new Duke. No one is going to put anything over on him, and I predict a new era of success for the family of the House of Este.

I was not that sharp during my watch. If it weren't for the indefatigable Count Villano, I would have wound up with a lot of egg on my face. Vince is different, and he won't require the nose of Count Villano to do his sniffing for him.

Nor will he ever have to call on the services of the infamous Peter Quinn to do some of the muscle work. Vince will find and break any enemies on his own. I could have used him too, during the bad times. Who knew?

I decided he didn't need any confirmation from me as to the fate of the misbehaving 'Malandrino'. It was best to leave his letter unanswered as an answer to his suspicions. Yes, the matter should rest with the 'Malandrino', wherever he is resting. As Vince would say. "Case Closed!"

When I did speak to him on the phone, I asked him how the wedding plans were going, and he so typically answered. "Why do men have to go through all this crap just to secure that special piece of ass?"

That was OUR Vince, our no-frills Vince. Incredible! Well, we men do have to go through all "that crap" if we want the women to believe that they are the "one and only" in any particular man's life... It is necessary for the female of the species to be assured and re-assured that she is treasured. There's no way around it if women are to function as serious mates.

"Vince, it can't go on forever, so bite the bullet and go through the ceremony. You may like it, after all. When you see Gilda all dressed in white, you're going to treasure that picture for all your of days. Believe me, I know. You both will be getting a lot of gifts, too. That's not too shabby.

Live with it Vince. It will be HER day, and all the days after that will be yours."

"As usual, there's wisdom in what you say. Well, my fate is sealed. So I may as well hunker down and take whatever comes my way."

"Now you're talking like a true Duke. Give it time. You're going to love every minute of it. Well, ALMOST every minute."

"Whatever it is, I'll handle it."

"That's for sure, I never doubted that. Vince, I'll ask you a special favor."

"Name it, Uncle."

"Take care of Regina. She deserves more than she got. See to it that she knows she's special, and that she is wanted and loved in the family."

"You don't have to worry on that score. She and Leonello are surrounded by love. She'll do well under your watchful eye."

"You mean under YOUR watchful eye. You're the man now!"

"I'll see to it that she's happy. Shall I try to find a mate for her?"

"Yes, in a little while. Wait until you think she's ready."

"Any special place to look for one?"

"Among the Monarchists. Join them, Vince. You'll need them and they'll need you."

"I hadn't intended to, but I see what you mean. OK, I'll do that as soon as I can; if I'm satisfied that it's a cohesive organization."

"Get Count Villano to sponsor you. That shouldn't be a problem."

"Right, I'll get on it right after the honeymoon."

"Any ideas as to where you want to go?"

"You bet! I want to show her New York City, then on to Niagara Falls, and after that to visit a certain Uncle in Florida."

"A capital idea! I'd love the company. You're a good man, Charlie Brown."

"Oh, Uncle, while I have you on the phone. Do you want to say anything about the 'Malandrino'?"

"He's being scolded by his mother just about now. Say nothing just yet. There may come a time when Regina will have to be told she's a widow. We'll cook up a story then."

Chapter Sixteen

"Operation Distraction"

Whenever plans for the wedding were being discussed, Vince would duck for cover. He told me that he's certain that women are all nuts. Yet, after seeing the wedding album of our wedding, he was happy enough to see that his wedding would be a much simpler affair.

"Uncle, I'm glad I don't have to go through what you did. That must have been painful."

"Actually, me and the other men went out on short trips and got away from most of it. It's true that there was a lot of pomp, and the royal uniforms were spectacular. Italy has not seen such a wedding until the marriage of the Prince Nicolo Pallavicini and Tinti Fusco and then not since. I think the days for those kinds of weddings are over."

"Lucky me! I wouldn't go through something like that for all the tea in China. I don't have friends that I can escape the Castello with, but I do like hanging around the repair shop to watch the mechanic at work. He certainly knows his stuff."

"Yes, he was a lucky find."

"He told me about the fight against the Red Brigade. He said he drove the car for Manolo on 'slumber night'. (The night the driver of the Brigade truck 'fainted' in his own bed.) Now, I would have enjoyed being there."

"It wasn't fun at the time, but it taught those terrorists something. They never tried anything like that again."

"Sure, after their leader 'fainted' too, they no doubt learned their lesson." That Manolo was something else!"

"Shhh! Not so loud. Someone may be listening on another phone. The less said about Manolo the better."

"Oh, right! Sorry! I lost my head!"

"How do you like your future in-laws?"

"They're very nice, and they seem to be quite happy that their daughter is taking such a giant step up the social scale. They are reveling in the attention all their friends and relatives are giving them. The Italians really feel that the Aristocracy is important, don't they?"

"Yes, and you'd better get used to it and start behaving like a Duke. Remember, you will be completely in charge and your word is law. Even the police will defer to you, as well as other professionals."

"I may begin to enjoy this."

"Good, but also bear in mind that you must always be judicious. Any signs of unfairness and favoritism will be noted, to your detriment."

"I shouldn't have any trouble with that. I think I'm fair minded as a rule."

"Then you'll be all right."

Two weeks later, Vince wrote:

My Dear Uncle,

I'm sure this will bring you a smile. If you could see the change in Gilda, you would laugh for sure.

Her sudden popularity in school has turned her head, and she fancies herself a super star of some sort.

Once the news got out that she is to become a Duchess in the House of Este her fellow students are flocking to her, and you can imagine what they are asking her. Many of them want to be her friend, and those that actually are, are making capital of it in every way, especially with bragging rights.

Gilda is really just a girl, so this sudden fame convinces her she's all grown up. I suppose it's only natural, but it also has had an effect on my relationship with her,

When she's at the Castello she continues to place herself close to me, and has given me permission to caress her breasts. Really! She's become quite brazen.

After talking to Aurelia, she has decided that perhaps she'll pursue a teaching career and has made several inquiries of local schools. Apparently she has forgotten for the moment that she'll be with child starting on her wedding night!

Her newfound confidence is such that Beatrice has cautioned her that the world is not the wide-open movable feast she thinks it is. Duchess or not, she will not be able to do everything she wants to do.

I find the whole thing quite amusing. Her parents are also trying to get her to put a lid on it. She'll learn the hard way. I'm sure.

Anyway she's still a sweet girl, never being overbearing to anyone, and still seeks the approval of everyone in the Castello.

A new group has formed comprising Leonora, Elena, Gilda, and even Carlotta. They have become as thick as thieves. It's all great fun for me. A regular show of shows!

As for me, I've been soaking in a cold tub! I don't know how long I'll be able to keep the fire banked.

Your Nephew, Vince

Dear Nephew,
I recommend you have some ice put into your tub. With Gilda and her parents living in the Castello, you don't have room for anything. For heaven's sake, leave her little titties alone! There'll be time enough for that.

It crossed my mind that you might put Deli in the Fusco manor and do some field inspections, but I'm sure you won't get away with that either. Senor Horny, I have nothing to suggest except to say that no man ever died from "Lacka-nookie".

Try not to show your horns! Women notice such things, and that in itself may lead to consequences. Cool it! Your uncle, Antonino.

Dear Uncle,

You were right about someone noticing my overheated state. Someone stole into my dark bedroom and took me into her mouth. I swear to you that I do not know who it was, and you must forgive me, but I can't bring myself to lock my bedroom door.

It only happened once, and perhaps it will not occur again. I confess it was done quite skillfully and it left me cross-eyed. Vince

I sent him a quick note:

Vince! LOCK YOUR DOOR! This weakness of yours is unmanly! Get it under control, now! Uncle Antonino

He must have done as I instructed, because I did not hear any more about this nighttime adventure. I'm perfectly content to leave his nighttime visitor a mystery lady, yet for the life of me, I cannot even remotely figure out who would have taken such a chance. If I were forced to narrow it down, I might vote for Regina, but I could be very wrong about that.

I did have a plan though. If there was any more noise about his sexual appetite, I'll have him on a plane back to New York City, where he can get his ashes hauled without causing any ripples in the family. I don't need any kinks in my plans for the new Duke.

I don't know what kind of husband he'll be, but I can only hope the pretty Gilda can keep him from getting the wandering eye. If his recorded adventures are any indication, he didn't seem to want to stray while he was working. When the time comes, I'll pass Gilda a little hint about keeping him busy on anything that can hold his attention.

She would be smart to get some others in the household to cooperate on this project. We'll start "Operation Distraction." Well, maybe it will not be necessary, IF he gets interested in every facet of the family business.

I was to learn that Gilda took "Operation Distraction" seriously, and much more so than the intention of my words, and much to my surprise and chagrin.

Chapter Seventeen

They are married!

Everything was quiet for several months at the Castello. The excitement shifted to the University of Bologna where the graduation ceremonies were being held. Beatrice reported how lovely Gilda looked in her graduation attire, and how she fairly glowed with pride and happiness.

Her doting parents were there and they presented her with a beautiful necklace. She showed it around and she also proffered her hand to show her graduation ring. She would shift that ring to another finger when the time came for her to have the wedding band slipped on to replace it.

The plans for the wedding were finished and all the arrangements were made with the church and the caterers. The guest list was very modest and consisted mostly of the Italian branch of the d'Este family, the Colonna family and of course the Villano family.

The two Nuns, my daughter Isabella and Elena's sister Monica were expected to be at the church, but not at the reception. There would be only two bridesmaids, Leonora and Elena, and Vince's best man was his cousin Peter d'Este from Manhattan.

Gilda's Maid-of-Honor was her best friend from the University, a girl named Veronique, who also graduated with her.

My daughter Beatrice would come with her man-friend Francesco, and I'll finally get a chance to meet him and find out what HIS intentions are.

Two Princes will honor the wedding. Prince Nocolo Pallavicini with his wife, my former ward Tinti, and Prince von Pappen would also be in attendance to show his respect for me. He attended my wedding when his daughter was Maid-of-Honor to my wife Laura and we in turn attended the wedding of his daughter Helga in Germany.

I arrived at the Castello in enough time to sign the papers making Vince the new Duke. Gilda will be marrying a Duke and she will immediately become the new Duchess.

I had to be fitted in a new tuxedo, the old one being strangely too small for me. Maybe it shrunk! It couldn't be that I gained weight! Really now!

We arrived at the Cathedral and although there was no publicity, word did get around so that there was a small gang of onlookers. There are people who will attend every wedding in the Cathedral. Just try keeping them away.

Only the Princes were in uniform. Prince Pallavicini wore his Navy Commodore's uniform with full regalia, including his ornate sword. Price von Pappen wore his gold cape showing the crest of the House of von Pappen, naturally.

All the women were dressed to the nines. They looked absolutely gorgeous. The bride stood out in her white wedding gown and flowing veil, and was as pretty as any picture ever painted by the masters of Italian Art.

When I caught Count Villano's eye, he had a mischievous look on his face. I wonder what HE was thinking.

Senor Colonna walked his sweet daughter down the aisle, and the tears in his eyes were unmistakably noticeable.

She was their only child, but he would soon forget his "loss" when he became a grandfather. It happens every time. They stepped along to the gentle music and when they reached the altar, he reluctantly raised his daughter's veil, and placed a fatherly kiss on her cheek.

Then, with equal reluctance, he handed her over to the handsome Antonino Vincenti "Vince" d'Este, Duke of Este, Count of Monte San Fele, of Lipari and of Emelia, and the new Lord of the Estensi.

Father Alessi, our family priest, officiated, and I never saw HIM looking so impressive, either. He certainly had enough vestments on to work up a sweat. He gave the mass in a clear voice and looked upon Vince and Gilda with a look of such divine love that it wouldn't have surprised me if he began an ascent into Heaven right there and then. When he finally joined them in Holy Matrimony, even he seemed to have a tear in his eye. Vince slipped the ring on her finger, and now they were one.

There was a reception in town at a nice hall, and the attendees ate dinner and danced to the music of a small orchestra. There were some speeches, and the best man told some raucous stories about Vince that were hardly true, but were calculated to amuse everyone there.

There were congratulations all around and Gilda blushed deep red when they started addressing her as "Your Grace". She hadn't expected that, it seems, or she didn't realize how strange it sounded when addressed to her.

Over at a side table Regina began to sob openly, and some of the women went to console her. She came close to being the Duchess, and it eluded her, and now she felt disgraced. Unbeknownst to her, she was also a widow. When one woman cries from happiness, another cries from anguish. It balances out, I guess.

Terzo was giving her a lot of attention, almost doting on her, as if he shared her agony and disappointment. It seemed as though Regina was especially grateful for his special attention.

Finally the cake was cut, and everyone was given a piece. Then the reception started to break up as people headed home or to the second reception planned in the Crystal Room at the Castello degli Estensi.

We all had a nice chat and some delicious drinks there, and soon the honeymooners were off to the Palazzo Estensi in Milano to spend their first night. Of course I wasn't there that night, but I can write what happened there as if I had a two-way mirror looking in on the lovebirds.

I was going to see them again soon after they went to New York City, then to Niagara Falls and finally to visit me in my villa in Florida.

After the kids left, I sidled over to Count Villano as said, "What were you grinning about? You looked like that cat that ate the canary when I saw you in church."

"I was grinning at you! I knew you were going to retire at last, but do you think your adventures are over?"

"All right Giulio, what are you playing at?"

"Just tell me honestly that you're not in the mood for a new adventure. Be truthful, now!"

"I have no trouble being quite truthful. Giulio, I've been enjoying the peace and quiet of my sunset years. There's absolutely nothing that you can come up with that will involve me in one of your capers. That's it!"

"You are far too young to retire. I understand that you took the loss of your Duchess Laura very hard, but it's time you began a new life. Come with me."

"Where to?"

"A few of us from the Monarchist Party are going to Switzerland to meet with the King. There are rumors that the Italian Government is considering letting the Royal family come back to Italy. How would you like to come along?"

I hesitated. The longer I hesitated, the wider his grin grew. Finally I said, "No, Giulio! You and your group go on ahead. I'm retired and my nephew is the new Duke, why would the King want to talk to me?"

"It's just a meeting! We'll have lunch and a glass of wine, that's all."

"Giulio, I cannot commit to anything. No, you'd better leave me out of it."

"The King has a long memory. Just show your face, OK?"

"How long will it take?"

"Now you're talking! I didn't want to go without you, my dear friend. I would have been bored."

I laughed, "Liar! You? Bored? That will be the day!"

And so I found myself in a small propeller driven plane on my way to Switzerland. We landed on a tiny airstrip near a huge house and debarked onto the tarmac. Some men came out to meet the plane, and they eyed each one of us carefully but said nothing. We were led into a large room with many chairs and tables, and I was easy to recognize the man who should be the King of Italy.

He rose as we came in and greeted us with a charming smile. He was none other than Vittorio Emmanuelle, the last claimant to the House of Savoy. Tall and balding, he nevertheless made an imposing figure.

We chatted about the efforts of the Monarchist Party's attempts to return him to the throne, but he demurred, saying that he would be content to return to Italy, and would gladly renounce all claims to the throne. "I just want to go home." He said simply.

Of course there are those who want to see the King reinstated, but they had ulterior motives. If a King were to be re-seated on the throne, they would sue to have all their original lands restored to them.

On the way back on the plane, I said to Giulio, "Too much time has passed. How can the Dukes hope to get all their land back?"

"You're quiet right. I would be impossible."

"This has a funny side to it. I never thought I'd meet the King while I was the Duke, and I meet him now that I'm no longer in power."

Giulio chuckled but said nothing. Then he said, "You know, Antonino, anything is possible!"

"I hope I don't read some day in the future that some people were involved in a plot of any sort. My friend, lasciammo il mondo come si trove!" (We must leave the world as we find it.)

Chapter Eighteen

A Honeymoon and a Street Fight

When Vince and Gilda arrived in New York they happily set about seeing what the city had to offer. There were the round of shows, fine restaurants, some museums, and visits to family and friends.

Vince took her to the New York tennis Club to show her off to his tennis buddies, but he couldn't play any games because his hand had not healed enough yet.

Lunch at the club was a noisy affair, and at one point the management cautioned that if they didn't behave they would be asked to leave. He had no idea who he was addressing.

They continued having a wonderful time in New York, and his family was competing as to who would get to dine and entertain Gilda first. His sister Francesca won out because she and Gilda had many conversations on the phone, and Gilda was the most comfortable with her.

I was able to get some rest when Francesca took Gilda shopping. Gilda had been to Venezia, Milano and Roma, but she was not prepared for the big stores in New York.

The last thing Vince expected was to have one of his old enemies track him down to his apartment house. The honeymooners were exiting the apartment one day and three men attacked Vince. Gilda was pushed aside and knocked down, but was otherwise unhurt.

Vince was fighting with his left hand, his right elbow and his feet, trying to avoid hitting with his right hand, which was still healing. He landed some heavy blows but was barely holding his own. He jumped up on the steps of the stoop and landed a few kicks, knocking a piece of pipe out of the hand of one of his assailants who was trying to hit him with it.

He was bound to lose the battle when help arrived. First, a neighbor picked up that piece of pipe and jumped into the fight. He was failing away at the attackers when the police arrived. They got into it with their Billy clubs, and the attackers soon were the worse for it.

An ambulance came to the scene and the medics treated Vince while the bad boys were loaded into police cruisers. A Police Sergeant asked Vince to come to the Police Station House to press charges.

Vince asked Gilda to go back into the apartment, but she wanted to go with him so they both wound up standing before the desk at the Police Station while the three men were booked. She stood right up to the Lieutenant behind the desk and told him in no uncertain terms that they were the Duke and Duchess of Este.

After seeing the miscreants locked up, Vince and Gilda were told they had to be in court the next morning, but Vince explained that the were on their honeymoon and the Lieutenant said it would be all right if he had his lawyer there to represent him.

Vince and Gilda returned to his apartment where he had to recover from his bumps and scrapes. Poor Gilda was beside herself, and did not know how to nurse anyone. She didn't know what to do, but Francesca arrived and took over.

A doctor was called to the house. Yes, when the d'Este family calls, doctors listen! He examined Vince and said the medics did a good job, and that Vince would recover in no time.

When the lovebirds traveled to Niagara Falls with Vince looking quite the spectacle, casual travelers they met wanted to know what happened, but Vince said. "My bride beat me up." Looking at the petit Gilda, nobody believed that but they laughed and let the matter drop.

All these details came to me in Florida, first by Francesca and then my brother Piero. I said, "Piero, will you look at this! On my honeymoon we had the fight in the Pecan grove in Uruguay, and Vince has a fight right in front of his house. Talk about history repeating itself."

Gilda was amazed by the waterfalls at Niagara, but was frightened when they went through the Cave of the Winds, which took them to the base of the falls. First, Gilda did not want to don the necessary rain gear, and then balked at walking through the tunnel.

Vince pointed out some children who were not afraid, and that made her decide to go through with it.

When the pair had seen enough, they traveled back to New York, where Vince had a doctor's appointment to check up on how he was healing. The doctor gave him a funny ball with which to exercise his hand. It was a soft ball that felt a lot like a woman's breast.

Vince didn't need the ball. He had two nice ones on Gilda he could exercise with. They spent a few more days exercising, then packed for Florida

When they finally got to Florida, Vince, still showing the marks of the fight, told me the story. Gilda proved to have a special talent. She was able to recite details of the fight that even Vince didn't know.

She described the whole thing from beginning to end and then said, "Do you see, Your Grace? I think I married a crazy man."

"Did you? How about the way he protected both you and himself? He did not have his gun with him so he had to use everything at his disposal. Even with a sore hand he held them off until help arrived. Does that sound crazy to you?"

"I don't know what to think, I'm not used to all this. Do you think there will be any more of it?"

"Not from those three men at least, I said. "Set your mind at ease and leave the heavy stuff to your husband. He will take care of anything that comes up, I promise you. You have a special man there, and you'll realize it some day."

"Your Grace, may I confide in you?"

"Of course my child! What is it you wish to say?"

"My Lord, he makes love with the same vigor that he fights with."

"Gilda!" Vince cried out. "He doesn't have to know everything!"

"Well, it's true my darling Lord! Isn't it?"

I was trying to surpass my laughter. Vince has a chiacarone (chatterbox) by the tail! Yes, and Gilda had a few more surprises up her sleeve, as we were to learn later.

In a few days a call came from the Police Department in New York City. An officer told Vince that he would not have to testify in court. The three men had bad records and the Judge sent them to the cooler for a nice long stretch.

Gilda enjoyed lounging around at the pool, but fortunately said nothing to the people there as to who they actually were. She had been asked to keep it quiet, and she complied, but almost split a gut trying to keep her mouth shut.

She didn't want to leave Florida in any haste, so she asked if they could stay a while, but alas, they had to keep to their schedule, and so I saw them off at the Tampa Airport, and they winged their way home.

Once there, they were picked up on the tarmac by Michele in the limo and whisked to the Castello. There they walked into a marvelous reception in the Great dining room. The ladies had gone to great pains to make it a special occasion, and of course they had the Witch of Endor, my mother-in-law, to show them how to do it.

That reception was the last hurrah! Now the business of running the family affairs fell to Vince, and the business of running the Castello fell to Gilda. She was going to have plenty of help, but who did Vince have, he moaned.

I told him he had me, Marco di Dante and Count Villano so he could stop complaining and get to his daily chores. He also had some very talented managers on the land, and workers who did their duties like machines.

Vince settled into it and began to function well or so I thought at the time. I didn't count on his restlessness and his desire for variety.

Chapter Nineteen

Babies, babies, babies!

My wife Laura and I slept in different beds most of the time. Vince and Gilda were going to sleep in the same bed. In my suite Vince had all the things he needed, but Gilda required her own movables to be place in there. Fortunately, the room was large enough so that it wasn't cramped at all.

It was Leonora who called and told me the great news Gilda was pregnant! Now THAT came as a big surprise! The Horny Duke didn't waste a minute. Gilda walked around the Castello like she was the Queen of the world. She couldn't be happier, and her parents, still living at the Castello were ecstatic. There was only one problem. She was having a very bad case of morning sickness

Vince was unable to bed his wife, and she moved to another room. Shortly after that, Regina and Vince began to console each other, and as a result Regina soon found herself to be pregnant as well, and for the second time.

Meanwhile, Vince was spending more and more time away from the Castello. He was attending to business, but he had a more personal reason for staying away. He was thinking of Leonora too much, and looking at her too much. She became aware of it, and it fired her own feelings.

Of course it was all impossible. It would be disastrous and they both knew it without ever saying anything or showing any sign of their mutual attraction. Life went on without anyone suspecting anything, and as always with sensible people, the matter became moot. Time heals all wounds? No, but time does calcify things. Personal feelings were no longer important.

It was fairly easy to figure all this out. I knew Leonora had fallen for Vince after the fight in the University parking lot, and I also knew Vince was distracted from his desire for Gilda.

But they, Vince and my daughter could be trusted not to act on any strong feeling they had for each other so I didn't concern myself with the matter, until I learned differently.

It was Regina who came to Vince's bed, and the matter of her pregnancy was not going to be a secret for long, if it ever was. I learned that Regina, instead of feeling shame, was quite happy with the fact that she was carrying Vince's baby. Sure! Why not? She had Gilda's permission! She, in her joy was going around the Castello kissing everybody, including the staff.

Vince told me that despite the fact that there were many months to go, everybody began choosing a name for the new baby growing within Gilda. "Leonora suggested Antonino, after you and me, and I suggested Piero after my father, but Gilda said everyone was being silly because she was going to deliver a girl!"

Jumping ahead in my story for a moment, that's exactly what she did! At first she wanted to name her Beatrice, after my daughter and her dear University mentor, but then she decided on Maria, after her mother, and Elena, after the dear lady in the Castello

The new baby was a happy addition to the Castello, but there wasn't the fuss that was made back when the Duchino Vincenti was born.

This was natural considering the history leading up to the two births. With my first-born it was so important to bring forth a boy who would be the catalyst between the two families. That was not a consideration now. There was time and Gilda would bring a boy into the Castello soon enough.

There was no such necessity to fuss or worry about. All the family had seen the original plan go sour when that first born proved to be an embarrassment to the family. Today the thinking has changed, and who knows maybe it will be little Maria Elena who breaks with the tradition and becomes the Duchess, and head of the House of Este.

Vince was a more modern thinker. Faced with his first born being female, he may just decide to name HER to the succession. Well, it's hard to change my thinking, but my time has passed and we are entering a brave new world in which capable women can lead just as well as men. (This was proven beyond doubt by Isabella Ganzaga d'Este, Marchioness of Mantua.)

Certainly another good example was Leonora, who did the work when it was necessary for someone with a clear head to step into the breach. Had I been a more modern thinker, I might have easily named her to the succession, but I think all will go well with the family now.

Then Regina delivered a boy! He was named Nino.

After several years of keeping company, my daughter Beatrice and Francesco della Rovere decided to get married.

The family got busy on another plan for yet another wedding, which then took place at the Cathedral in Monza. They found a nice house near the University campus and made Bologna their home city. They produced no children.

One can come to the conclusion that theirs was an intellectual marriage.

The following year Gilda gave birth to a boy. This time there was more of a fuss because now there was a new Duchino in the Castello. We all sensed that Vince would name him to the succession in later years. He was named Piero the Second, so that was the certain sign that the baby would be the next Duke. He was named Piero II.

Vince wrote:

Dear Uncle,

Regina came to me and asked if there was any way we could find Vincenti. I explained to her that after so long a time, if he wanted to come back to her he would have found a way.

I further speculated that he may have found work on a ship and was living the life of a carefree sailor. She didn't agree with that idea, saying Vincenti was too lazy to look for that kind of hard work.

She did some speculating of her own. She pointed out that to the north of Uruguay were the deep jungles of South America. "Perhaps he found his way to one of those tribes and is living among them."

I told the unfortunate girl that she should forget him and perhaps look for another husband. What do you think? Can you find a suitable husband for her? She will never be happy until she is married again. Leonello can enjoy the influence of a father that way, too.

Also, Gilda's parents seem to have settled into the Castello and are not planning to go home anytime soon. Gilda likes it that way, but I'm not sure I do.

I await your opinion on these two issues, Vince

Dear Vince,

You handled that well. I suggest you tell Regina to wait a while longer. After enough time has passed, you can have her marriage legally annulled, and she'll be free to marry then. You and I know that the new suitor will not have to worry about a long-lost husband showing up to once again embarrass the family.

Whatever you do, never tell her she's a widow. She will want to know how you know that, and the feathers can hit the fan. And don't give her another baby!

Meanwhile, Leonello and Nino will grow up in the Castello and we can claim them as ours. We want men in the family. It would be a good idea to keep

Regina on a string until Leonello and Dino are of age, and perhaps we can give them good positions and keep their loyalty forever.

If Regina remarries, her husband may want to adopt them and absorb them into HIS family. No way! They are OURS. Let's keep it that way.

Allow Gilda's parents to stay as long as they please. They are nice people and are respectful as well. Remember, Gilda is an only child so it's important she feels secure in every way.

Besides, there's enough room in the Castello now to accommodate not only her parents, but her graduating class as well. Just joking!

Your uncle, Antonino

That's how a Duke has to think. His arms must encircle the whole of the family, the land and the workers. Vince must learn to be more possessive and even greedier in the right way. He must think in terms of owning everything, and putting it all in his pocked.

He is the Lord and Master. The Duchy, if we can call it that, is his entirely and personally. It is in this way that he can command and make it work. He must not think in democratic terms. That could lead to dissention and chaos. For a Duke to be a Democrat is a contradiction in terms. The successful family speaks with one voice.

It is, however, incumbent upon him to weigh each problem carefully and to always be fair. To be arbitrary can lead to dissention as well. He must develop the maturity to be right for the family when quick decision have to be made.

For example, in any case involving trespassing, he must act quickly and firmly to discourage it, using force if necessary to protect the family. No Mister Nice Guy when it comes to strangers and interlopers. He must be prepared, even to kill, when someone enters his domain illegally.

Not all men are cut out for this manner of leadership. It takes a special man, and that's why I chose Vince. The elimination of Vincenti was calculated to make Vince's job easier. I saw no other way.

Chapter Twenty

A Hunter of Men

After the brief affair between Vince and Regina, Vince went on a manhunt. I mentioned earlier in this narrative that he was never content to allow the Bergamo gang to extort money from the manager of the Buono land.

Quietly, secretly, and with no one in his confidence, he prepared to deal with that problem. His plan was to handle it alone, as was his practice when he worked as a Bounty Hunter in the United States.

When it was over, he called me and said that there was no longer a problem in Bergamo. I stopped him from talking on the phone and asked him to send me a full report. This is Vince's report:

I used the information Count Villano had given you some time ago to get the names and locations where these extortionists could be located. He said they frequented a men's club, and were in the habit of leaving for home late in the evening.

I further read the manager's reports as to when they arrived at the Buono manor house, and the amounts of money extorted from him.

I knew I had to work in total secrecy, but at the same time I needed a driver who would take me to Bergamo, then after I found a hiding place to operate from, would bring me food and pick me up when the job was finished. Andrea Astuzia, our mechanic, was the ideal person.

I said to him, "I understand you drove the car for Manolo on 'Slumber night.' How would you like to drive me on a little adventure?" He was all for it.

He was not being told what the project was, but only that he would do some driving in the middle of the night, and that it was to be a secret mission. He was ready for anything.

As a Bounty Hunter, I never went after anyone with the idea of killing him, but this case was different, and frankly it sickened me. Nevertheless, I could not let the extortions go on, especially because there was the overhanging threat of our wheat fields "accidentally" catching fire.

I planned as carefully as I could. The work had to be effected silently and quickly. We went to Bergamo, and after looking around I found a good hiding place behind a store. I set up some fruit boxes and made a little hut where I could spend the day, then do my creeping around at night.

Andrea went back to the Castello, but forgot where my hiding place was, so I was stuck with not only reconnoitering how to assassinate the gang, but how I was going to eat when my food ran out. I won't go into how I scrounged my food. It's too disgusting even to recite here, and my toilet habits were even worse!

I placed myself across from the men's club at night and saw that the gang members didn't always leave at the same time. Good! There was one problem. I wasn't sure who was guilty and who was innocent.

Looking through the window of the store with a pair of opera glasses, I saw that there were five men who always sat at one table. From the descriptions given in the manager's reports, it was clear that those were the men I was looking for. It was time to act.

That night one of them left, and I followed. As I approached him from the rear, I noticed that the buildings in that street had cellar airshafts with either just bars or with metal covers.

I covered the man's mouth with my gloved left hand and the stiletto went into his side. Then, pulling him back, my second thrust went under his ribcage and into his heart. I 'rolled' him to make it look like a robbery, then found an airshaft I could open, and dumped him into it.

The information I got from his wallet said he was Cosimo Schietto. That was enough for one night. I headed back to my hiding place, and threw up along the way. I hoped I wouldn't get too sick to finish the job. Strangely, no one working in the store noticed my hiding hut. The pile of boxes looked the same, but I had a tunnel in which I could crawl in and sleep

The next night I followed two of them. I hit one of them with the stiletto, and the second man just stood there in disbelief, even as I rolled the first one.

I told the second man to help me feed his friend down an airshaft, and he DID it. I then dispatched and rolled him and fed him down the shaft to keep his friend company.

The second man was Santo Citterio, and the third Abburzzi Faro, known as "L'Imbicile" No wonder he just stood there.

The stiletto I was using had a very thin blade and a sharp point. Anyone could see that such a weapon had only one purpose; sticking! I was jamming the knife with such force that I'm surprised the blade didn't break. The Italians know how to make good stilettos.

On the third night there were the last two. They seemed to be totally unaware that their friends were not in attendance. As I followed, the first man turned into a building and went down a few steps and into a basement door. I went after the other one. He turned at the corner with me close behind, and as I did the job on him I saw a woman walking on the sidewalk across the street.

She started running, and I rolled my quarry as quickly as possible then back-tracked the way I came. Surely she would call the police. Seeing the basement door where the other man went in I thought to hunker down in the shadow of the stairway and wait for any police cars to pass.

To my surprise, the basement door was unlocked. What good luck for me! I eased quietly inside and thought this a good place to hide. Then I saw a dim light and went toward it. There was my man leaning over a worktable and counting money.

He was easy! I left him slumped over the table, grabbed his wallet and the money he was counting, and then waited. There on the table was a book. It turned out to be a list and money record of his victims. What a bit of luck that was! I didn't want the police to get their hands on that.

I couldn't go out into the street right away, so I waited, but hunger drove me to slip up the inner stairway and into the man's kitchen. More luck! I found something decent to eat.

I sneaked around looking for some kind of valise and found a leather bag that would do nicely. The woman sleeping there never heard a thing.

Back in the kitchen, I put the money, the book and the other loot into it, and packed it with more food.

When I thought it was safe, I left the building and went toward my hideaway but changed my mind. I had to get OUT of Bergamo, not hide any longer.

I got to a phone at first light and called the Castello, and when I got Andrea. I gave him the coordinate streets where I was and told him to get his ass over there fast. He would be a while, so I ate some more of the food I liberated from the kitchen.

When he arrived, I got into the car and we raced home. I never reprimanded him, nor did I enlighten him about the time I spent in the city, but he did look askance at me when he saw, and smelled, the condition I was in.

Dirty and unshaven, and stinking like a skunk, I sneaked through the Castello around the back way and gained my rooms. After the most refreshing bath I ever had, I checked the last of the wallets and found that I had eliminated the 'boss', Salvatore Mancuso in his cellar, and his lieutenant, Angelo Costa, on the street.

There has been no noise about this in Bergamo or anywhere else, Can it be the police did not connect these killings together? That's the oddest thing about the whole affair. Or maybe it was a question of 'Good riddance' for the police. Vince

When I read his report I called to tell him that I was angry at him for putting his life into such a dangerous position, but at the same time I had to congratulate him on an incredible job well done.

"You certainly are a professional. I don't know anyone who could have pulled a stunt like that. You must promise me you'll never do anything like that again."

"I can promise that easily. I was sick the whole time and I don't think I will want to do that kind of hunting ever again. Now I want to live the quiet life"

"That's what I like to hear."

Later, Vince paid the manager of the Buono land an "innocent" visit and learned that no one came for the tribute money. So far so good! While I was there I told him to change the landscape around the manor so that the wheat wasn't growing too close to the house. He understood.

Chapter Twenty One

The bird coops

If the reader has read one of my previous books, "An American Duke in Italy" then he knows about the strange structure that stands in the property just north of the Castello. No one has ever figured out what it was designed to hold, but it may have been built to stable passing cavalry horses.

Historically, that's the idea that makes the most sense. The roof had long ago disappeared and any wooden separators within have also gone, probably used for heating. Anyway, Vince has decided to put a roof on it and section it off to raise birds!

Not just eating chickens, but some exotics as well. He has a fondness for peacocks and pigeons as well. I told him I didn't think pigeons would be advisable if he didn't want to start cleaning the roof of the Castello.

Then he thought of building a pond to raise some ducks, but again I told him that there would be a smell, and the quacking would keep some people awake. I didn't mention the calling of the peacocks. That is a pleasant sound.

Then I suggested raising bantam chickens, and he liked that idea. Not only were they interesting, but they would produce little eggs for the table.

This would be Vince's new hobby, and would take his mind off thoughts and feelings he had no right to harbor.

He and Leonora had to work closely together, so any distractions would be for the better.

Vince decided to put a roof on the "barn" as we now called the structure, and while he was at it, he laid plans for a new entrance to the Sala Romano. His Idea was to use it as a place for visitors instead of the small reception room on the second floor of the south wing. That way, visitors would not be trampling through the Castello itself, and only the family could reserve the reception room on the upper level.

The Sala Roman, so called because Giulio Romano painted the center oval on the ceiling, could be used by the staff as a recreation room in bad weather when it was not used to entertain visitors.

The Crystal room would be used for state business.

The birds would take up only half of the barn, and the other half would be used to house the extra cars and the farm vehicles for the winter. At last, Vince found a sensible use for that odd building.

To the surprise of everyone, Gilda's father took to the idea of raising the birds. He took it on himself to set up the western half of the huge "Bird Barn" to build roomy cages for canaries and parrots. He told Vince, "We can scour the world for really exotic birds like the cockatiels and other fancy birds."

Vince didn't want to go overboard, so they concentrated on the basic collection. After a while they saw that the hobby was producing a lot of birds, so they decided to go into the business of raising selling them. Vince gave his father-in-law the go ahead to make a business out of it for himself.

When orders started coming in for birds they didn't have, he went and got them and started raising those exotics too, so that the variety of birds became quite large. There was no talk about going overboard anymore.

Now the Bird Barn needed more attention. Some areas had to be heated and even running water had to be supplied. I began thinking of making a trip to Italy just to see the new barn. Photographs showed it to be quite an interesting place.

Another problem arose. As word got around, people wanted to come to see the bird barn and the exotic birds that were being raised there. They began to think of it as a zoo or a live museum. Arrangements had to be made to give tours to these visitors.

Even members of the household wanted to have canaries singing inside the Castello. Sorry to be corny, but that whole area in and around the Castello was beginning to be "for the birds!"

Remember, we also had wild birds visiting the Sunken Garden too, especially after a heavy rainfall, so at the right time of year some tours were arranged to see those waterfowl too, quietly so as to not scar them off.

Vince was going public, and I warned against enemies who may want to sneak in and do harm. But I wasn't in earnest. The days of the Red Brigade were over. At least I hoped so. Anyway, I was sure Vince could spot any neer-do-wells in the crown, when he was at home, that is.

Vince began traveling after that. He visited the Villa Laura often, and also took several trips to Uruguay. He took trips to foreign countries, ostensibly to sell our products, but I suspect it was also to ease his mind about a certain cousin with whom he was in love.

He also took trips to his native New York City and stayed in his apartment for two or three weeks on end. He was the Duke, and he could do as he pleased, but this was heading in the wrong direction.

He may have taken some romantic pleasure on these trips, but I really can't say. Sadly, he had that weakness. It was bound to have consequences. Gilda and her parents began to ask questions, and Leonora brought the situation to my attention.

Chapter Twenty Two

Playing the Field?

Once again I had to warn Vince that his sexual appetite was getting out of control. "Vince, you're beginning to stray big time, and this is unacceptable even for a Duke. I want you to get back to the Castello and stop this wandering."

"Didn't you tell me that once I was the Duke I could do as I pleased?"

"Yes I did say that, but I also said that you had to eschew anything that would hurt the family. Vince, your aunt and I were married for forty one years, and I never found it necessary to go to another woman. You cannot convince me that you're needs are greater than mine were."

"Uncle, I'm just used to variety!"

"You had enough variety when you were single, as I did. The need for variety is all in you mind. There is no physical necessity for it. You must get back to Gilda before you hurt the family."

"How would the family be hurt if I slip out for an occasion piece of strange?"

"Two reasons. First, you took an oath to be faithful, forsaking all others." Second, you haven't read the small print in your contract. I have the legal power to take the ducal title back!"

"I didn't read that in the contract!"

"No, you idiot1 You didn't read that because I had that stipulation inserted in the small print when I saw that you were too horny for your own good and the good of the family."

"Well that was certainly a sneaky thing to do!"

"Wasn't it though? Now put your thinking cap on. You know you can't fool me, so it's time to pay attention to your ducal duties. What do you say?"

"Gilda is not enough for me!"

"And you can't have Leonora either! What's it going to be Vince?"

"What do you mean?"

"Look Stupito! Don't play games with me or you'll be back in New York and working as a Bounty Hunter. Make mistakes and you'll face the wrath of your father, or worse!"

"Or worse?"

"Yes, don't force me to do anything severe, Vince! For Heaven's sake, THINK! You have enough information to think about what I'm saying. I will protect the family no matter what I have to do. You are right for the job, but you have to control where you pecker goes."

"This is not a development that I expected."

"Well, what DID you expect? The power I have placed in your hands comes with responsibilities. If your behavior gets outside the family we can face ruin. Oh no, Vince. That will not happen. You can bet your very life on that!"

"That sounds like a threat!"

"Really?"

"All right, Uncle, Give me a few days. I'll decide as to whether I can be good, or if I'll resign. Is that satisfactory?"

"Yes! If you decide to resign, you come away with nothing. NOTHING!"

"I'll call you in a little while."

"Don't take too much time!"

Now I understand why Count Villano was laughing at me. He has a better grasp of the younger generation and knew I would not enjoy my retirement long.

If I have to take back the titles, all four of them, then I may as well plan to move back into the Castello. I'll have to see to Gilda and the two children if Vince decides to resign. What have I done to deserve this?

As I waited for Vince's call, I spoke to Leonora and explained the crisis.

Leonora said, "I can't understand why he should be unhappy here. He has it so easy, yet he's making it hard for himself."

"Daughter, is there anything you think I should know about?"

"No father. I DO feel love for him, but there is nothing going on and nothing you or I should ever be ashamed of. I love and respect both you and Gilda, and the children are so precious."

"Thank you Leonora, That's what I wanted to understand. You are so precious to ME, and it's so good to know that you're on the right side of this matter. Vince is a good man for problems, but I never anticipated that HE would become one."

"Father, give him a chance! He's just having some growing pains, and Gilda is still a bit naive. I'll talk to her parents about the advice they might give her, but don't hold out much hope there, because they seem to be quite naïve themselves."

"Let me know if that plan works out. If not, I'll talk to all three of them. If Vince decides to go back to the Castello, have Father Alessi talk to him. Maybe Vince will profit from some spiritual strengthening."

"That would surprise me. Vince may throw him out!"

"That will kill two birds with one stone."

"I'm not sure of what you mean, father."

"I mean that I'm not too fond of Father Alessi either."

"Oh, Father, how can you say that? He's is truly a saintly man. Honestly, he is, and you must have seen that yourself. What do you have against him?"

"I believed he cost me your sister Isabella."

"Oh, THAT! Father, Isabella is very happy. Can't you accept that?"

"I've accepted that. It's just that I wanted her at home with me. It's selfish, but that's the way I felt at the time."

"Well father, that's old history. We have to fix the situation with Vince."

"Amen to that! I should hear from him soon."

"Let me know, father. I hope he'll stay here."

"I do too."

"By the way, he has intentions of getting Isabella and Monica out of the convent."

"How can he do that?"

"I don't know, but he'll find a way, if thee is one."

I heard for my brother Piero, Vince's father. "Antonino, I read my son the riot act. I told him that if he resigns the title, I'll disown him and he will never be welcome in my house. My daughter Francesca gave him the same ultimatum. She was even more vehement than I was. She scolded him for thinking of abandoning his wife and the children to come."

"Piero, I have hope that Vince will get over this temporary madness. Let him call me, and we'll come to some kind of agreement."

"I appreciate that. He must do his work and he must do it in the proper way. I thought he was raised better than this."

"I'm confident he'll come to his senses. It hasn't been easy for him. He gave up what he wanted to do, for work he didn't want. Once he realizes, finally, that he's in a key position, he'll do the right thing."

"I hope you're right!'

"Ill bet on it!'

"That's good enough for me. Antonino, I didn't like the idea of your inserting that clause in the contract saying you cold take his titles away from him. He has taken on a huge job. Why should he have this sword of Damocles hanging over his head?"

"You don't think that was a good idea given his weakness for women? You and I have been faithful in our marriages, and as far as I know except for Vincenti there hasn't been any cheating. Are you suggesting we give Vince license to cheat?"

"Of course not! Does this provision hold until your death?"

"No. It also provides that proceedings can be started by a family member under certain extreme conditions after I'm gone."

"Well, you certainly are careful. You cover all the bases, don't you?"

"You can bet on that too. I'll brook no fooling around, even after I'm in my resting place. Vince must see it through and have the right stuff to train your namesake, little Piero for the succession. We must continue to look far into the future, and there's no room for selfishness."

"Well Antonino, I defer to your decisions, as I always have. Let's pray for luck."

"Yes, we'll pray for luck, and make the necessary moves to insure it."

When Vince did call he was contrite. "Uncle, I've been in the wrong, and I think I can go back and do my job now. I'll give up my apartment here in New York so that I won't be tempted to come back here."

"Keep the apartment! The next time you want to see New York, take Gilda with you. It's that simple."

"Yes! You're right again. Thank you uncle, I'm on track now. I'm heading home."

"Good, Vince. Go and give that girl a bunch of cute babies. Wear your shoes to bed and make boys!"

Chapter Twenty Three

Enter Andrea di Savoia

When Vince arrived at the Castello, everyone was happy to see him. No one but Leonora knew about the conversations that occurred between her and me. Vince was able to start again with a clean slate, and once he began looking around he saw one thing that had to be changed right away.

The Bird Barn was attracting too much attention, so he decided to move it. If it was going to be a business, he thought that it should operate in a city environment.

He began to look for a likely sight, and finding nothing in Monza, went to check Bergamo.

He found a nice large place there. That was good, because now he could check on it and the wheat fields outside of Bergamo (the Buono land) on the same day. This meant efficiency. He was proud of himself.

Once the business was moved, Gilda's father didn't want to be out of it, so he and his wife moved to Bergamo to take care of it. That was an unexpected bonus that Vince took credit for. Now Gilda will have to mature more quickly without her doting parents around to lean on.

I was concerned that Vince would begin to have the same problems I had with my wife, the Duchess Laura. She would defer to her mother, Countess Colonna for just about everything, even as I tried to convince her that SHE was the Duchess, and outranked her mother.

Fortunately, I was wrong. Gilda remained sweet and pliable, but began making her own decisions. Leonora never bucked her but only taught her how the system worked. The Contessa stayed out of it, and Gilda did not have that problem to deal with. She never knew how lucky she was.

Seeing how Gilda was functioning also helped Vince to appreciate her more. Would he fall in love with her eventually? He'd have to be made of cement not to.

Gilda did not want her babies too far away from her so they slept in their cribs at night near the master bed. Vince didn't mind, and often got up to see to them when they complained. During the daytime they were in the nursery under the watchful eyes of their nurses. Gilda kept HER eyes on the nurses.

The way Gilda took to her babies is one of the marvels of the female of the species. She was over them like a clucking hen, and saw that her helpers did the same. She was not going to be a part-time mother that was certain.

Maria was active, but Piero was a sleepyhead. If he wasn't suckling or pooping he was sleeping. That was fine with Vince. He wasn't ready to buy Piero a football yet anyway. The baby should get all the sleep he needed now. When he became the Duke, he would not be getting that much, Vince reasoned.

According to the information I got from the Castello, Vince was going to be a better father than I was. I let the women take care of the children. I had my own problems.

Vince looks in on them, and even plays with them. He would have little Maria giggling and wiggling, but not so

Piero. He would just look at his father as thought he was trying to figure something out, some kind of puzzle.

The Castello settled down for a nice long period of peace and quiet. So it seemed. Every once in a while Vince and Leonora would cross paths, often when no one else was there, and their eyes would meet and lock on each other.

One day Vince whispered, "Just one kiss!"

Leonora said. "Don't be a fool! Do you think one kiss would be enough? We must NOT start! It will end in tragedy."

"What are we to do?"

"Nothing! Find a distraction, Vince. You have enough to do."

Leonora again asked me if I could find a husband for her. I understood her dilemma and said I would do what I could. My initial inquiries had to be among the members of the Monarchist Party. I started with Count Villano.

"Giulio, I hate to think of it, but it's time to find a suitable husband for Leonora. Alas, we can't keep our children babies forever, and Leonora has grown up. What does the crop of young men in the Party look like?"

"The trouble is that the young men are matched up early. You may have waited too long to make inquires for Leonora."

"So she marries a man younger than herself, what's wrong with that?"

"Nothing, but there are none. There's a widower, a relative of the House of Sforza, but he's older, a trifle heavy, and has three daughters. Don't look to him!"

"No, he wouldn't make a good candidate; I don't want Leonora dealing with anything like that."

"Why the rush now, Antonino?"

"She's been mistress of the Castello, and now Gilda has taken over, so Leonora should have her own life and family."

"Is there a problem?"

"That's the problem, Giulio! I can't really say. Leonora has told me that she should have a husband, but beyond that I can only speculate."

"I see! She distracted! OK I'll get right on it. Any abjection to someone outside of Italy?"

"I guess not. Do you know anything?"

"No, but it would help if I knew you didn't object to a foreigner. It gives me greater latitude."

"I don't think we should limit ourselves. There are some good men out there."

"Yes, I agree. I'll get back to you."

"Thank you Giulio. I'm out of it now so I can use any help I can get."

"Should I talk to Vince?"

"Not yet! Let's see what you can come up with first."

"Right! Stay well, Antonino."

"You too, Giulio!"

It didn't take Count Villano long. When I picked up the phone he fairly shouted. "Bingo!"

"Bingo? What do you know about that game, Giulio?"

"Nothing, but isn't that what Americans say when they hit the winner?"

"Yes! What winner did we hit?"

"There is a young man about Leonora's age living in Italian Switzerland and is a relative of the House of Savoia. In fact his name is Andrea di Savoia. He is unmarried and his passion is the piano. Shall I extend an invitation for him to visit the Castello?"

"Yes, indeed! Notify Vince that Andrea wants to call upon Leonora. Make it sound like its Andrea's idea. Can you do that?"

"I can! That's good thinking on your part. I'll make sure Andrea learns about Leonora first so that there will be no surprises. You must call Leonora and say you may have found the perfect husband for her. Give her something to think about."

"Gulio, you're an absolute genius. I'll do that now, and thanks for your good work."

When I got Leonora on the phone, I asked, "Is this La Signora Leonora di Savoia d'Este?"

"Father? Are you quite all right? What are you babbling about?"

"Plans are being made to have one Andrea di Savoia visit the Castello to meet you. You can expect a letter from his family any day now. How's that for fast action?"

"Father, what do we know about him?"

"Not a lot. They live in Italian Switzerland, and have kept a low profile. Andrea is a pianist, but the main thing is he's single, and you did say you wanted me to find you a husband, did you not?"

"Yes, father, I did, but I didn't think you would act so swiftly."

"Are you changing your mind?"

"Oh, no! Let's have this Andrea visit by all means. You do remember that I wanted to stay in the Castello. Will he live here?"

"I don't know! Don't go speculating. When you see him, ask him."

"All right father. Oh my! I must take time to catch my breath. Is he coming soon?"

"Again, I don't know! Relax, Leonora! You're only going to meet him. You've welcomed many people to the Castello before. Treat this as just another visitor. If you like him, then we'll talk about what to do. All right?"

"Yes, father. I'd better see to my wardrobe."

"Good idea! Get yourself something nice." That ought to keep her busy for a while. Females! Are they really of this world?

Chapter Twenty Four

A Dance of Fire?

Somehow Vince either was not notified, or had forgotten about it, so when the call came from Count di Savoia, he was taken by surprise. The voice on the phone identified himself, and then asked, "Is this the Duke of Este?"

"Speaking!"

"Good morning Your Grace! My son Andrea can call upon your daughter Leonora on Sunday afternoon. Is that all right with your schedule?"

"One moment, Count. I'm not sure I know what you're talking about. Leonora is my cousin, not my daughter."

"My apologies, Let me speak to Duke Antonino please."

"My uncle is retired, I am the Duke of Este."

"I see! Well there need be no confusion. If it's all right with you, my son can be there on Sunday to call upon your cousin so that they might become acquainted."

"He will be most welcome, my dear Count. We will be happy to see him."

"Thank you, Your Grace. I hope they like each other. It is a singular honor to be invited to the House of Este."

"The honor will be ours, I'm sure, Count. It will be nice to meet your son."

"Thank you, Your Grace. You are most kind."

Vince called me and reported this phone call. He seemed genuinely surprised, and asked if something was going on that he should know about. "This man di Savoia thought he was talking to you."

"He's just not up to date. The books won't show that I have retired, and the news of your marriage and your succession may not have reached into the remote towns of Switzerland. Things like this may happen for a while until you succession becomes general knowledge."

"What's this about Leonora?"

"Vince, it's time she had a husband. Count Villano told me about Andrea, and he feels he is right for her. I hope we found a good man. If Leonora has her way, they will live in the Castello, so chances are we won't lose her to Switzerland."

"Uncle, as the new Duke, can I oppose this union?"

"Yes, but why would you if they like each other? He's an aristocrat and the right age. If he's good looking, then what's the problem?"

"Well, I just want the chance to look him over. We don't want to make any mistakes for Leonora, do we?"

" No, but she has a good mind, She can decide for herself. Don't sweat it, Vince."

Am I listening to the voice of jealousy here? So far Vince handled the Count di Savoia well. If I see any interference into Leonora's life, then I'll have to take steps.

I can trust Vince to protect the family and its interests, but in this one area he has to be watched. His appetite ranges too far for anyone's good. He has been accustomed to taking what pleasures he desires from women he chooses, but Leonora is definitely off limits.

They have had eyes for each other, from all indications, and Leonora herself asked for a husband realizing the potential for a scandal.

Vince is in the position of being able to interfere, and most likely for his own purposes. At this point, even if Leonora marries Andrea di Savoia and continues to live in the Castello, would this prevent them from connecting in some future date?

No! The danger will be ever present, and in the Castello, where there are so many cavernous rooms, many unoccupied, could they not meet and fall together?

Leonora must marry and move to Switzerland. Yes, she must leave her beloved home and get out of the situation. Vince must stay on the job, so Leonora, much as I hate the idea, is the expendable one.

First, let's see if they like each other. At the moment we're putting the cart before the horse.

When Andrea di Savoia arrived at the Castello the first thing one noticed was that he knew how to dress. He looked magnificent in his finery, Leonora reported, and the first impression was a good one.

He in his turn complimented Leonora on her own attire. She described what she was wearing and made her own first impression on Andrea. We were off to a good start.

Vince did not. In fact when Andrea came, Vince was out with the field hands, despite it being a Sunday, and came in with dusty shoes and smudged clothing. Andre looked at him, and did not know he was looking at the Duke until he was introduced.

He bowed and said, "Your Grace!"

Vince did a quick check on him and said, "Well, aren't YOU the dandy!"

Andrea pretended he heard nothing and smiled tolerantly. This man was a gentleman, and Vince needed a minute for that to sink in. He collected himself and said, "You must excuse me. I'll need some time to clean up. I'll see you at dinner." And without as much as a by-your-leave, went to his rooms to bathe.

It was Gilda who took up the slack. "Welcome to the Castello, Senor di Savoia. We shall do our best to make your visit a memorable one. Please have a seat. We shall have our aperitif here in the Crystal Room.

Andrea looked around and marveled at the appointments in the room, and expressed his appreciation. "We have nothing like this at home," he said. Then he invited Leonora to sit near him, saying, "If I may be so bold, may I ask you to sit next to me, Signorina? Excuse me, but perhaps I should be asking whether I may sit next to you."

Leonora, most pleased by his attention and gentleness, smiled and blushed, but sat right next to him on a settee. She was taken with him, but would she like him enough to consider a marriage?

Gilda asked him about his career as a pianist and concertista, and he shyly told them what he had been doing in that area, and finished by saying that his concerts were only local shows and that he did not know if he would ever gain international attention.

He was a modest man, and quite a contrast to the bold Vince, who by this time had dressed up and came into the crystal room. The first thing out of his mouth was, "When will we eat?" He wasn't making any points with anybody.

Dinner was a very nice affair. Pains were taken to make it special, and anyone who knew could tell that the Countess Colonna had a hand in it again. All the special finery was trotted out, and the room prepared to look like Kings ate there.

Again one could see that Andrea was impressed, but this time he said nothing. Fortunately Vince was gracious, no doubt remembering some of the things he learned at his mother's table, and they all enjoyed a pleasant time.

Afterward, they repaired to the smaller reception room on the second floor, and Andrea was asked to play something on the piano. He was good! He played some light Sonatinas, but finished strongly with De Falla's "Ritual Fire Dance"

Elena, who was the only other person in the Castello that played the piano, was entranced. (No one knew that Vince played also. He said nothing about it.)

Who knows, but Elena may have fallen in love with the dashing Andrea right there and then. We must remember that Elena was of marriageable age as well, and may have wished for a man like this for herself.

Vince asked Elena to play, but she said she couldn't after what they just heard. She was a shy girl.

From what I gathered, romance was bouncing off the walls in the Castello. Ordinarily this would have been a wonderful thing, but on this night, all the wires were criss-crossing and who could know how it would all finish?

And Vince was not the one to untie all the knotty problems that may result from all these mixed feelings. No! He would only add to the problems.

Gilda saved the day again. The Duchess of the Castello suggested that they leave Leonora and Andrea alone to get better acquainted, and the rest of us went back to the Crystal Room to get comfortable while we waited for them to join us.

Elena went to Vince and asked him to find HER a husband, but Vince said he didn't know how to proceed on that and would she write to Duke Antonino instead. She promised she would.

She wrote with such a tiny hand that it was not too easy to read:

My dear Duke Antonino,

As you no doubt have heard, Andrea di Savoia came to call on Leonora and the family, and he made a good impression on all of us.

Do you think I'm ready for marriage? I did not think to ask before because I have been so content with my life here, thanks to you and your goodness. However, after seeing the handsome Andrea, I think I would like such a man for my husband.

Would it be difficult to find such a one as this for me? Like Leonora, I would not like to leave the Castello, so perhaps my new husband would not mind living here too.

I would be content with any living accommodations, as long as my new husband would be comfortable here.

I am well aware that I'm just a silly dreamer, but Leonora and Andrea look so nice together that I feel womanly stirrings that are quite real.

Please tell me, my dear father, do I deserve a handsome Prince?

With love and respect, Elena.

When I called her on the phone, I assured her that she was indeed deserving of a handsome Prince, and that I would try my best to find her one. I did not want to call Count Villano again, but I had no choice. I was out of the picture now, and relied on him to know who was who in Italy and Europe.

He laughed loud and long. "Antonino, you're missing all the fun! Come back to Italy join our revelries. You've had enough of the quiet life. Come back!

"As to a husband for Elena, that is possible, but I don't know if I can discover another Andrea di Savoia! This might be a little tougher because, while Elena is a d'Este, she does have a difficult background. You know how the families are! They want to be sure of every connection. I'll do my best."

"Thanks Giulio. You know, I have been thinking of returning to Italy. I just may do it."

"That would make a lot of people happy. Would you keep Vince here?"

"Yes. He's the Duke and the bodyguards all rolled up into one package. Why, do you have anything against him"

"Oh, no! He's a fine vigorous man. Maybe a tad too vigorous, I'm thinking!"

"What are you trying to tell me?"

"Nothing really. He's an American. What can I add to that?"

"Giulio, I'm an American, too! So?"

He laughed heartily. "Do you want me to add to that?"

"What's this? Well, perhaps I shouldn't ask!" and I joined him in his laughter. He was right. I wasn't much of an Italian when I first went to Italy. He had to take me by the hand and lead me around.

Chapter Twenty Five

Fanning the Flames

Leonora and Andrea hit it off nicely, but I was not sure Vince was getting used to the idea. He wasn't being difficult really, but he wasn't exactly as cordial to Leonora as he was before. She was hurt by it, but didn't confront him because she knew what was ailing him.

Vince continued to be nice to Gilda, and he certainly was giving her enough exercise. Gilda, in her innocence bragged to Leonora, Regina and Elena how strong Vince was sexually. She hardly suspected that she was only fanning the flames of curiosity and desire. Regina agreed with her and they laughed about it.

Nor did she fully understand the capacity Vince had for bedding other women. She should have been enough for him, she thought. She certainly was accomodating, but was still approving and allowing Vince to give Regina an occasional "touch up"

In less than six months Andrea proposed to Leonora. She accepted him, but she did so out of the knowledge that she had to leave the Castello, and this marriage was her way out. He was a nice man and acceptable, but she did not love him.

Although the mansion Andrea lived in was huge by Swiss standards, it did not compare with the Castello, and it pained Leonora greatly to leave her home. They were married in Switzerland, and Leonora moved to the mansion.

The Castello suddenly seemed vacant! Everyone missed her and Vince felt betrayed, an emotion he had no right to feel. He liked Gilda very much, and she pleased him very much, and Regina was great in bed, but he loved Leonora! It may have been at this time that he made himself a vow that some day he would possess his cousin, even if for only one connection.

Vince was not an evil man. He was of a type, and what can be done about it? How many stories do we know of such frustrations? Questa e la vita! That is life!

I asked Villano if modern day women would help each other out that way, and he said, ""It wouldn't surprise me. All the old rules are out, Antonino. Life is getting interesting, isn't it?"

"Giulio, I feel so OLD!"

"You're not, but our fight is over! Let the young ones sort it out."

"Where will it end?"

"You can stop complaining. If Regina brings another boy into the Castello, will you mind all that much?"

"No! You're right! Ah me, what are we doing, Giulio?"

"Have faith. It will all work out in the end."

Chapter Twenty Six

The Rock of the Estensi

A letter came from Leonora:

My Dear Father,

I have not wished to complain to you about how much I miss the life in the Castello, because Andrea is such a dear man, and his family has treated me royally.

There is one matter that is causing me some concern, however. My dear husband does not seem to be potent. He tries, and I try to help, but I'm not sure I know what he needs.

He is manly up to a point, but then he fails. Is there a doctor who can help this condition? I believe I should be on the way to motherhood by now. I do so want a baby.

Sorry for bringing you this problem, but I don't know whom else to talk to. If this becomes common knowledge, I'm afraid I'll be the one derided for this failure.

I'm homesick, father. I would like to go home for a while, May I? Would it be proper?
Leonora

What could I say? I told her it would be all right to go home and see her family but that she should bring Andrea for a brief vacation. He could use a change too, and it may do him good and even help him in some way.

And so Leonora and Andrea came to the Castello for what was supposed to be a week, but stretched into a month. It must have had a salutary effect on Andrea, because a short time after they arrived back in Switzerland Leonora found herself inciente!

Yes, she was with child. Andrea was totally surprised by this, but he supposed that one night he had somehow found the strength to finish what he started. I think he's a simpleton, but that's neither here not there. I only hope the baby is healthy. There could be a problem with birth defects when first cousins join in the primary act of concupiscence.

The coincidence of her pregnancy and her visit to the Castello was not lost on me. With Count Villano's words still in my ear, I decided to let the universe unfold in its own way. Hands off! That's the best way now.

In the final analysis, what do I know? It will always be the smell of the wick, I suppose. I throw up my hands. I was faced with a 'fiat accompli' and that's all there was to it, but is that guy Vince going to knock up every woman in the Castello?

I had yet another disquieting thought. Did my baby Leonora plan it that way? When she heard that Regina was pregnant, did that give her the idea that she might save her marriage by having a baby of her own? Is it possible that the love she felt for Vince was the impetus for it?

Of course no one will ever know. At that exciting moment when Leonora and Vince joined together in heat and passion, did Vince regard himself as the Master Lover, never thinking that he was being used to further a designing woman's ends?

I believe, now, that my daughter has a better understanding of things than all of us put together. It was she who saw the needs of the family when Vincenti failed in his duty, and she saw the needs for her marriage when Andrea failed to make the grade toward fatherhood.

Vince was getting more and more adept at taking care of his domain. After Leonora's visit, he seemed to have grown in stature, and in addition became a pillar upon which all the family and its businesses could rest.

He never asked Count Giulio Villano for help although they did become friends. He never sought to hire anyone to protect the family, and he never again called for a family conference.

Of course there was speculation about the killings of Senor Mancuso and his hirelings, and of course there was speculation about how many children he fathered, but no one ever challenged him.

Each person who dealt with him soon found out what niche he or she was to fulfill, and did what had to be done. The House of Este never ran as smoothly as when Vince finally picked up the reins.

He never joined the Monarchist Party, but he did follow my lead in one respect. He gave modest dinners for family, friends and neighbors, but never threw a party.

He stopped sending money to the convent where my daughter Isabelle and Elena's sister Monica lived as nuns. He also stopped giving to the church, but he raised the salaries for the staff and the workers.

He limited the maintenance on the Castello to just what was necessary. No frills for Vince. He did one thing for himself. He found a nice wall out of doors where he could hit a tennis ball against, and spent hours smacking the ball around.

The old cook who once chased me out of "her" kitchen was fired, but when she broke down and cried, he re-hired her, but he was the boss from then on. When HE walked into the kitchen she was ready to serve him. He goes there once in a while and teases her and banters with her, and she knows it's all in fun.

He never impregnated a single woman. Only married ones! Elena was never bothered, and maybe she wondered why, I can't say. Given his personal aura and strength, she would have readily given in to him had he wanted it.

Even the beautiful, redheaded Velia, the secretary's assistant was never approached.

We never did find a husband for Elena. Her misfortune followed her and none of the families would consider her as a good marriage prospect for their sons. They would change their minds quickly enough if they knew how wealthy she had become.

For my part, I never feel the urge to go back to live in the Castello. It's enough to know that everything is in good hands, and when my time comes I will finally rest beside my beloved Laura, and that's all I want now.

When I meet her in Heaven I won't have to explain why I sent Vincenti to her. I think she'll understand.

Gilda became the perfect wife, mother and Duchess. She was not as naïve as I had originally thought. She recognized that she was married to an Italian Stallion, and what do smart horse riders do with stallions? Why, they let them RUN, that's what they do! And that's what she did.

Vince ran until he'd had enough, then settled down and found out that pulling the marriage wagon was not such a bad job for a healthy horse.

It was the old Countess Francesca Colonna, my mother-in-law, who did not like the new situation in the Castello. While I was not surprised at receiving a letter from her complaining about things, this was one time when I had to admit she had a point. She had a firm hand that made the very words seem as angry as she was:

My Dear Antonino,

I have been quiet about this long enough and can only say that if this behavior on the part of the new Duke continues, I shall have to institute a lawsuit to have the Title restored to you.

The attorney tells me I can do this, and Vince's behavior has been abominable. He has turned the Castello into a Bordello!

I do not want to stir up a storm here, God knows that there have been enough of them under your watch, but if this doesn't stop someone will have to take action, and apparently you will not.

You must not accuse me of having an overactive imagination, and I'm not making any of this up! You know I'm right when I say that Vince has been having his way with some of the women here.

Don't pretend that you don't have at least some suspicion that I'm right. He has fathered Regina's son Nino, and there is every reason to think that they had several connections, not only one! Who knows, he may be still joining with her!

I have seen and heard enough to say that Leonora has also given in to him. I cannot imagine your "baby" consenting to such an unspeakable union. That her husband could not impregnate her is no excuse.

To add to the horror of the situation, I'm certain that the Duchess Gilda not only knows all this but also had consented to it. Oh, you should see what great conspiratorial friends they all are!

Vince has fathered four children right under this roof with four different women, and where will it end? Will he start making the rounds with the maids?

Antonino, you have been the power here for so many years, Are you going to surrender to the upstart? For Heaven's sake, do something!

Countess Francesca Colonna Malatesta

Well! I didn't know my mother-in-law descended from the House of Malatesta! No wonder she was always so stubborn1 Now SHE complains of the behavior of Vince d'Este? She should read her own family history. Gad! What a bunch of troublemakers THEY were! One of the Malatesta Dukes married a d'Este woman, and then killed her when he found her in "flagrente delicti.".

Her rhyming, though, amused me. "He's turning the Castello into a Bordello! That's poetic!

I called Vince. When he got on the phone, I read him the Countesses letter and asked him point blank if there was any truth to it. He didn't hesitate in saying there was! I had to marvel at him. This guy really has balls!

"Vince, I thought I had your promise that your would stay only with Gilda. Why did you lie to me?"

"Uncle, I didn't lie. That was my intention, but Gilda asked me to service first Regina and then Leonora. Let me explain. It all seems to have started when Gilda bragged to the other women that I was a strong sex machine.

"One day Regina begged Gilda to lend me to her so that she may be serviced. This was at the time when Gilda was sick during pregnancy. Regina was beside herself with desire. She threatened to go find ANY man so that her fires could be slaked, but Gilda thought that would be untenable, so she asked me to do it.

"Regina has not been greedy. It is rare that she comes to me with open legs, and I don't make a lengthy thing of it, giving her just enough to bank the fire.

"Leonora also had Gilda's permission, but in her case it was because she was desperate for a baby. We went to bed twice, once when she arrived at the Castello and again before she left. She wanted to insure that she was fertilized, but never intended it to be an extended romance.

"Uncle, you must believe how close these women have become. They are fast friends and will help each other in every way, even to the point of using me to solve their problems. I don't pretend for a moment that I found the whole thing disagreeable, and I have felt a strong love for Leonora for some time, but it's just about over now and things have settled down."

"I cannot believe this. My Leonora submitting to you so that she can have a baby? This seems like a tall tale."

"When Gilda left us alone Leonora reminded me of the time I asked her for just one kiss. I told her I did remember that, and also that she told me, 'Don't be insane! Do you think one kiss would be enough?'

"Then right at that moment, she said she would have that kiss NOW! Uncle, I have no excuse except to say that we were in love. You knew that and hastened to find her a husband."

"I cannot listen to any more of this. It is monstrous!"

"Just one more thing Uncle, then you can dismiss me as you will. Leonora did this to save her marriage, not to have a fling. Please be convinced of that."

Well Count Villano did tell me that this was a new age, and we agreed to let the chips fall where they may. Oddly enough, the more I think about it the less I can find fault with Vince. He may have been willing, but he was also being used. But incest? This is truly hard to accept.

I told Vince at the time, "See that you behave as a moral man and a Prince of the House of Este. Clean it up, Vince. You're in charge of things. Do you want others to follow your example? Think of the children."

"Everything will be all right now."

"See to it!"

"Uncle, Regina must have a husband, and Leonora is very happy with her little Isabella. "I'm sorry if you are disappointed with me, and disconcerted over what has happened but believe me, it is not something that will continue. I never wanted to let you down."

He's a rogue and a horny toad, but you have to admire the guy. He's not afraid of anything! If I were to walk upon the scene now, I would be afraid of HIM! There's no doubt about it, he is the true head of the family, the Rock of the Estensi

Chapter Twenty Seven

All the little feet!

And the children, you ask? Marie Elena, the perky Duchessina was growing up thinking the Castello was hers. She wandered everywhere and had something to say about everything, and the old Countess loved her! They are birds of a feather, I'm sure. It's so amusing!

Piero III, the Duchino was quiet, but made friends easily. He grew up loving the land, and the people who made it work. Something in his mind told him it was what he had to do. Vince took him everywhere so that he could see it all with his own young eyes. He would be a man of the land. The soil of Italy would be his clay, to mold as he would. There will be no failure here.

Regina's first son, Leonello was shy and modest. He looked up to Vince as his father figure, but his brother Nino could look up to Vince as his real father. Well, what difference did it make?

Leonora gave birth to a girl and she named her Isabella. She was growing up a contented child, patiently trying on all the dresses her proud and overbearing mother bought for her. She looked shockingly like Vince, but no one ever mentioned it, to my knowledge. I was happy enough to have another Isabella in the family, even though she would grow up Swiss.

After a time, Andrea di Savoia was able to father Leonora's second child, a son, which they named Nicolo.

Prince Nicolo Palavicino was so flattered that he sent a truckload of gifts to Andrea and Leonora for the baby's use.

Should I have taken Vincenti out on the land the way Vince takes Piero? Would it have changed the history of the House of Este? This question will gnaw at me for the rest of my days, but I had my hands full at the time, so perhaps I could not have done all I should have with my firstborn.

Quietly, the Countess Francesca Colonna Malatesta, my mother in law, my wife Laura's mother, and she whom I often called "The Witch of Endor", died in her sleep. She went peacefully, but during my watch as the Duke, she caused me a lot of turmoil with her constant dissention.

Fortunately, after her husband died, she mellowed and became a valued helper to all in the Castello. I never thought I would say it, but the old lady will be missed. As is so often the case, we never realize a person's contribution until we no longer have it.

The new Duchess Gilda learned a lot from the Countess during the latter days, lessons the Countess saw the young Duchess needed and she was willing to teach.

She seemed strong and determined, and no one suspected she was ill. The countess complained about everything else, stridently and loudly, but I can't remember her ever complaining about her own health.

She was not a d'Este, but I asked that her remains be placed in the crypt with the passed members of our family. Vince overruled me, saying that she was best laid to rest next to her husband. Carlotta, her daughter and Laura's sister, agreed with Vince.

One day, soon after the Countess's determent, Carlotta went to Vince and suggested that now, with her being the only Colonna left of the old family in the Castello that perhaps she should move out.

Vince would not hear of it. "You are related to Gilda, and I ask you to stay and continue to feel at home here." Needless to say, Carlotta and her husband were happy with Vince's attitude, and so they stayed, ever being a pleasant part of the household and family.

The reluctant Vince went on to become a stronger, better Duke than I ever was. Count Villano continued to maintain a pipeline into the Castello, and could tell me with some precision what was going on there.

He reports that Vince, now running with the bit in his teeth has instituted ideas and procedures that even the strict secretary, Marco di Dante applauds. Vince looks into everything, but with a kindly and benign leadership that has everyone at ease and eager to please.

Vince has become a farmer. What a far cry from his former life, when he was a sort of tennis bum, and a murderous bloodhound of a Bounty Hunter. Those weeks he spent under cover and alone, searching out Senor Mancuso and his gang, were the last of the old days and the old ways.

He was a contented man, enjoying the company of an incredibly smart and tolerant wife and two wonderful children. Yet no one around there ever thought he had gone soft and could be taken advantage of. He still exuded that animal strength that warned others that he was like a coiled snake, ready to pounce.

Of course it was too much to expect that nothing would ever happen to stir up things in the Castello. At this time Vince decided to make an important change in the building.

As you read in "An American Duke in Italy", The Sala Romano was a large room on the first floor of the north wing of the Castello, and in recent generations that room had fallen into disuse. Vince decided on a bold plan. Make an outside entrance to the Sala, with a patio and an overhang, so that the room could be used for visitors. This would prevent visitors from having to trudge to the second floor of the south wing to the small reception room.

Now, the upstairs reception room would be private, and used only by the family. The main reception room, the Crystal Room, would be used for matters of State.

Construction was started on the Sala Romano and the necessary bathrooms and cloakrooms, when the Castello was taken by surprise but the sudden move of Regina to the Villa Laura to live with Terzo!

It happened this way. Terzo had asked Vince if the woodsman who was sent to Uruguay for punishment with Vincenti could be sent back, since he needed him. Vince agreed, thinking that the man had been an unwilling tool of Vincenti's scheme in the first place.

When Regina heard that the woodsman had returned, she wanted to speak with him about the fate of Vincenti. Vince decided to tell Regina a big lie, saying that he had just received news from Count Cesare in Uruguay that

Vincenti had drowned while swimming, and was buried there.

She did not cry. Instead she decided that if she were indeed a widow, she would go to live with Terzo. She knew he wanted her, so it looked like a sensible move, all things considered.

I agreed with Vince that they would have to marry, and so they were, in a simple service in the chapel of the Castello.

The clever Regina, having failed to become the Duchess d'Este, was satisfied to become a Contessa in the House of Este.

In time Regina had another boy, which was named Luciano. So, she had her first son, Leonello, by her husband Vincenti, her second son, Nino, by Vince, and her third son, Luciano, by her second husband, Terzo!

Quite a merry mix-up, I think you'll agree.

The boys grew up in a nice environment and under the care and watchful eye of their father, Antonino III d'Este, called Terzo. One nice thing was that they all were fathered by a d'Este, so there was no confusion there.

Their visits to the Castello were always an occasion for much merriment, with the now happy Regina being the prime mover. When the new crop of children got together, it was an occasion to behold. Luckily, The Sala Romano was ready to accommodate all the children when it became an indoor playground for them and the staff.

When not being used for guests, the room could be a place where the staff could relax and play table games or do their sewing and knitting. Some bathrooms were installed where the stable used to be, and the area included a warming room for when food was being served, the main kitchen being all the way over on the south wing. A second kitchen was out of the question.

On the patio, people could sit and watch the stars at night, or do some bird watching during the day. The only sore spot was that odd building where the birds were being raised at one time. Maybe a wall would hide it.

There had to be an extension of the driveway and a parking area for the guests. I liked the plan and the thinking behind it. Terzo came over and put in his two cents, and his ideas were incorporated in the construction.

When all the children were there at the same time, it was a gathering to behold. Maybe I'm missing something.

Epilogue

I want to use up my bragging rights concerning my nephew, Antonino Vincenti d'Este. It wasn't easy, but my choice for the succession worked out very well, although not exactly as I envisioned it would be. The family will be on a strong footing for many years to come, although a trifle too colorful. Yes, all in all, I must say that I'm rather proud of myself!

My wish is that when times change for Vince, he will adapt to those changes better than I did in my time. I have the feeling he will, since he is so much a part of the force that is making those changes. Did he ever fall in love with Gilda? I think so, judging how they stuck together even on the smallest projects.

Looking back, I must have seemed quite the stick-in-the mud to my family, but I did my best and they did not suffer too much for it. The difference between me and Vince is that I had to learn on the job, but he seems to have known what to do even before he got there.

He never joined the Monarchist Party, which is an indication of how he planned to go his own way.

As a leader, I followed the rules as best I could. As a leader, he MAKES the rules! Look out, everybody while Vince is walking about his domain!

Il mio lavoro e finito!

Antonino Vincenti d'este

www.ingramcontent.com/pod-product-compliance
Lightning Source LLC
Chambersburg PA
CBHW080920180426
43192CB00040B/2564